A GUIDE ON HOW TO
CALM DOWN

QUICKLY. EFFECTIVELY.
BEFORE YOU DO OR SAY SOMETHING STUPID.

C J Kruse

Absolute Author
Publishing House

A GUIDE ON HOW TO CALM DOWN

This book is a work of fiction. Names, characters, places, and incidents are products of the author's imagination or used fictitiously. Any resemblance to actual events or locales or persons, living or dead, is entirely coincidental.

Publisher: Absolute Author Publishing House
Interior Designer: Dr. Melissa Caudle
Cover Design: Design Pro
Author Photographer: Author Selfie

Library of Congress Cataloging-in-Publication Data
Kruse, C. J.
A Guide to Calm Down/ C. J. Kruse
p. cm.

ISBN-13: 978-1-951028-10-7

1. Self-help 2. Self-Improvement

0 1 2 3 4 5 6 7 8 9

DEDICATION

To my family. Thank you for your love, support, and patience in me.

TABLE OF CONTENTS

INTRODUCTION

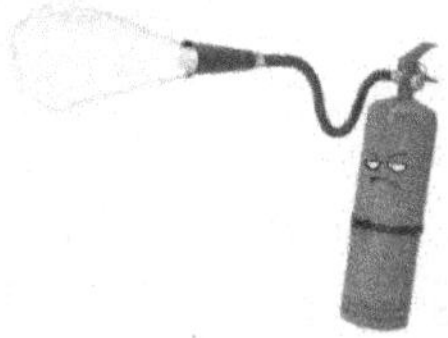

Do you ever get worked up? Do you ever find yourself knowing that if you don't pull yourself together quickly, you might snap? Burn a bridge? Ruin a relationship? Say wounding words that can't be taken back?

If so, one thing is certain -- these moments are crucial. In them, you have a small amount of time to get back your clarity. To get back in touch with your sanity.

Sure, you'd feel much better after taking a warm bubble bath or playing a round of golf. But, by then, the crucial moment will have passed, and you will have already embarrassed yourself. You will have hurt somebody's feelings. You will have crossed that proverbial line to a place there may be no coming back from.

The good news is that you aren't powerless. You don't have to just sit there and wait for those negative events to transpire (as you know you've done before). There are ways to calm down right now. In this moment. Quickly. Effectively. Before you do or say something stupid. That is what this book aims to teach you how to do.

A short time ago, I discovered the need for this book. I was going through a personal battle and was more worked up than I had ever been. I wanted to lash out at the people I love. Drive off in my car and never come back. I knew I had only two choices; pull myself together or do damaging things that could haunt me the rest of my life. Fortunately, I decided to make the smarter choice.

I got on my phone and reached out to a few friends for advice, but some of them didn't answer. Others did but weren't sure what to tell me. The person that I thought would be of most help, only told me that he didn't feel qualified to give advice. I hung up the phone, feeling truly alone.

I then turned to the internet for answers but quickly discovered how little helpful information there was for me in my exact situation. I couldn't find a single book about calming down. All I could find were anxiety books, anger management books, and relationship books. None of them approached the subject directly, or as their main topic of focus.

Even the self-soothing books I found were for babies. I wondered... is calming down something that only infants need? Isn't it something that grownups need too? And, unmarried people? And, what about those of us who can't call ourselves sufferers of chronic anxiety? Why isn't there any literature that doesn't exclude people who don't fall into these other categories, but still want to get better at mastering their emotions?

In my frustration, I suddenly realized that I needed to make my own book. A different kind of book. One that didn't spend as much time talking about babies or marriage or mental health and cut straight to the subject of calming down.

I sat down and began writing all that I could. I wrote about what was going through my head when I was feeling excited. All the questions I had. All the things that made me feel better. And, the things that didn't. I tried to figure out why certain remedies were effective and why others weren't. I wrote about who I thought was causing the problem, and why I thought they were to blame. What I felt compelled to do and say, as well as how I had felt in the past after acting on such impulses.

I articulated my frustrations as well as I could, constantly adding to what I had written. I was developing better ways to handle my frustrations. Slowly but surely, I started to feel more prepared. Better equipped. Now, after all of my hard work, I can finally say with honesty that I'm better than I was before.

Don't get me wrong. This doesn't mean that I've turned into Gandhi. I still wrestle quite a bit with this. There are still plenty of times when I blow it. Times when it feels impossible to calm down. Times when I just don't **want** to calm down. There are even times when it takes me hours, days, or even weeks to see (and admit) that I handled a situation poorly. But I'd rather be honest with you about that.

I'd rather not approach you proclaiming to be a guru, or as though I stand on some lofty plateau with the answer, and as though you're just some lowly simpleton for not knowing it. I also don't want to make this struggle sound easy, because it's not. It ***IS*** a struggle. But, victory lies in knowing that. And, in being honest enough to admit it.

Because, here's the truth -- no matter how much ground I gain at this, and no matter which tall mountains I climb, each new frustrating situation presents a brand new (and sometimes impossible-seeming) challenge, requiring all that I have to return to my saner, calmer self.

So, if your goal truly is to get better, take heart. I believe this book will help you just as it has helped me. It will give you a better understanding of your struggle, as well as an edge on handling it. Because, if these solutions are good enough to work for a normal guy like ***me***; they should be good enough to work for just about ***anyone!*** Are you ready? Let's get going. I can't wait to share what I've learned with you!

THINGS WE WILL TALK ABOUT

- Why we get worked up -- the triggers that make us crazy.
- What it means to truly calm down (rather than pretending or going through the motions).
- The reasons why it is *so important* for us to learn how to calm down.
- The reasons why it is *so hard* for us to actually do it.
- Myth debunking -- tackling common misconceptions.
- The importance of prevention -- Learning to catch yourself ***before*** you get worked up.
- The stuff we normally try (and why it doesn't work).

- The stuff that ***does*** work -- Helpful, practical ways to calm down -- Physically, mentally, or with the use of natural supplements.

Right now, if you happen to be worked up, looking for immediate remedies, simply skip ahead to the chapter, titled: **THE STUFF THAT WORKS.** There, you will find some useful tools for helping you calm down in this moment. Otherwise, if you can wait, I suggest that you continue reading this book through in its entirety. The knowledge and understanding you acquire along the way will only add to your likelihood of success.

Here is a short list of benefits that you have to gain by reading this book and learning how to apply what it teaches:

- Knowing how to calm down can increase your happiness. As you become calmer, you'll be more emotionally present. You'll be able to enjoy your moments because you'll actually be in them. You won't be trapped inside your head, fixated on some past or future concern.

- Knowing how to calm down can increase your physical health too, which is closely tied to your emotional health. It may actually do more for you than the vitamins you take, the gym membership you pay tons of money for (but rarely use), or the time you invest reading nutrition labels on the foods that you eat.

- Knowing how to calm down can make you more attractive. Because, when you're worked up, your appearance changes. Your face turns red, your eyes reveal the negative emotion you are carrying, and your veins bulge out of your neck and forehead. Let's just say... it's not your best look.

- Knowing how to calm down can actually improve your IQ. It unlocks your creativity and your problem-solving capabilities that are bound captive when your pulse and mind are racing.

- Knowing how to calm down will help you keep what you hold dear -- those things like your marriage, your career, and your life savings. Things that take years to build, but only a single careless second to lose.

- Knowing how to calm down will lessen the chaos in your life. Not because it will solve all your problems, but because it will help you see them more clearly. Think about them more logically. Calming down is the solution that makes you better at finding all the other solutions.

- Knowing how to calm down will make you more efficient too. Because, with a calmer mind, you'll be able to focus on your real goals, rather than being distracted by all of those silly side-goals, like getting revenge, winning dumb arguments, or achieving vain objectives that mean nothing in the grand scheme.

- Knowing how to calm down will also minimize the regret in your life. It will give you a sense of control. It'll make your life function more smoothly, drawing more people to you who want to work alongside you and be a part of your team. It will make you a better communicator. People will actually notice your message, rather than just the messenger. Of course, there are many more benefits, and you will pick up on them as we go on.

On this journey, I hope this book will be your ally. At times, it will probably make you angry, as it may step on sensitive nerves. Other times, it may make you laugh, as it attempts to push you forward with tough-love humor. It will sometimes be that pat on your back that you desperately need. Or, that swift kick in the pants that you need even more.

It contains solutions that are possible, but not easy. No miracle-cures are offered here, and nothing in this book should be seen as an alternative to any medications you may be taking. All that I talk about here is fairly simple and made for everyday application. But, it is based on one small assumption -- that you are a fairly normal person. By that, I mean that you have your own best interests in mind, as well as the best interests of those you care about. You don't fly off the handle regularly, continually, uncontrollably, or without cause. If that doesn't describe you, then this book probably isn't for you. You need a different book. And, most likely, the help of a professional. This book is meant for learning how to calm down quickly in normal life situations.

With that being said, let's carry on (if you haven't decided to jump ship). I think you will find a wealth of practical, useful information here. I even venture to say you will enjoy it.

And, if you take the content seriously, I believe it could mark the beginning of a new chapter in your life.

WHAT IT MEANS TO BE WORKED UP

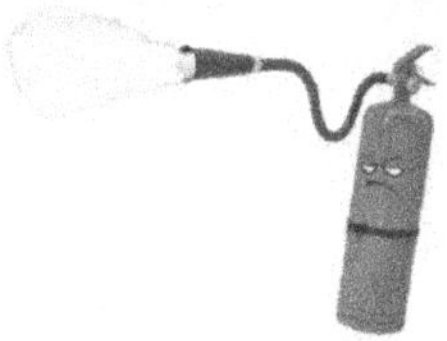

To start, let's talk about what it means to be worked up. What do you think of when you hear this term? Maybe, a certain memory comes to mind. Or, a movie or television show where one of the characters gets bent out of shape in a humorous way -- Inspector Dreyfus in The Pink Panther, Ralph Kramden in The Honeymooners, or Doctor Leo Marvin in *What About Bob*.

There seems to be something comedic about seeing somebody get worked up. Maybe, because we can all relate. We've all had something, or someone get under our skin and irk us to the point of insanity. A drippy faucet. A slow driver in the fast lane. A friend who always shares his opinion when it's not welcome.

Those of us who live in close quarters with other people tend to develop short fuses with them over time. Our roommates, family members, and spouses seem to step on the same nerve over and over. Eventually, heightened sensitivity develops. The smallest offense can easily send us into a tizzy.

The dictionary defines being worked up as "Being emotionally aroused. Excited." We might simply classify it as a reaction that most average people have during stressful moments in their lives.

We'll often describe a worked-up person as being:

- Frazzled
- Flustered
- Discombobulated

We might say that his:

- Chains have been rattled
- Gears have been ground
- Goat has been gotten

An expert, of course, would use much different terminology. He might describe him as:

- Aggravated
- Bothered
- Exacerbated

An expert would also be able to describe the physiological changes taking place in a worked-up person's body, such as:

- An elevated heart rate
- Elevated blood pressure
- Dilated pupils

But it usually doesn't take an expert to spot a worked-up person. Most of us can spot one simply by looking. We see it in the furrowed brow, the clenched fists, the pacing, or the nervous fidgeting. The telltale signs that a person's mind has wandered elsewhere -- that he is physically present but mentally absent.

Of course, not everyone displays such visual signs. Some of us wear a poker face that betrays what's going on inside us. We are so good at hiding our emotions, that we even hide them from ourselves!

Last year at your daughter's birthday, your daughter came up and asked you, "What's wrong?" You insisted that everything was fine, even though hindsight showed you... she was right. You were frowning in every picture. Apparently, you weren't really over that argument you'd had with your spouse earlier that day.

Getting worked up has the characteristics of a cycle -- it has a start, a middle, and an end. It is something that isn't easy to stop once it gets going. As Author Charles Duhigg describes in The Power of Habit, it is sometimes as though we must "finish a frustration" once it starts.

There are many emotions that can get us worked up. Sometimes, they are good emotions, like the kind you get when your boss gives you a raise, or when your tax refund was bigger than you expected. You crank up the stereo and roll down the windows, cruising down the road feeling high.

Usually, though, we don't like the emotions behind our excitedness. We feel angry, frustrated, or irritated by some problem. Perhaps, because we were arguing with our spouse, or because our kids were trying to see how far they could push us.

Fear is another unpleasant (and common) emotion. It's the one we're feeling when we are cornered or facing some threat -- real or imagined. When we sense pain or embarrassment or the loss of control coming, we take flight, or we become aggressive and combative.

Shame can also get us worked up. We are often more embarrassed by how our wounds make us look than by how they make us feel. Shock, sorrow, and anxiety can also get us worked up. Or, anything that causes us to panic.

While there are many emotions that can get us worked up, they all seem to have one thing in common -- they all affect our ability to think, act, and make decisions. Even the good emotions can make us susceptible. They can cause us to make promises we can't keep or pursue unrealistic goals.

Being worked up causes us to act less intelligent than we are. It makes us forget what we know about life, what we want out of it, and whom we care about in it. It makes us forget how much more to it there is than the temporary way we are feeling.

Quite often, being worked up is the only real problem we are facing. The problems that we think we are facing exist only in our heads. And yet, this is still a problem, because even the things we imagine can hurt us. False alarms cause real panic. Irrational phobias put people into real hospitals. What's in our heads rarely ever stays in our heads; it has a way of escaping and manifesting in real, tangible ways.

The real danger in being worked up has to do with more than just feelings. It has to do with the unproductive ways our feelings cause us to respond. Or, the way they cause us to freeze and do nothing when we should be responding.

Very often, getting worked up is the thing we do right before we do some other stupid thing. It is the precursor to some of our most unproductive behaviors, including:

- Panic.
- Impulsiveness.
- Shouting.
- Excessive arguing.
- Aggressiveness.
- Disruptiveness.
- Mean-spirited attacks.

Can you think of more?

But, maybe no one needs to tell you this. Maybe, you already have a shelf full of your own stories to tell about times when your emotions caused you to make poor decisions. Don't worry. We all have some, and there is absolutely no need to justify yourself here.

This book assumes that you have good reasons for getting worked up. Great reasons. Maybe even the best reasons. It assumes that every time you have ever overreacted, slammed the door, punched a hole in the wall, driven off angrily, or called somebody a name, the feelings prompting you to do so have been valid.

So, rest assured... that part of the problem has been solved. I mean... the part that involves helping you feel good about yourself in the wake of dumb choices you've made. Now, comes the hard part... changing. Coming up with an actual solution. Though this will be more difficult, it is the only thing that will actually improve your life. And, give you fewer blunders that you feel the need to justify!

CALMING DOWN

What does it mean to calm down? Does it mean sitting down Indian style with our eyes closed, humming some Gregorian chant? Does it mean squinting really hard and repeating some pointless mantra over and over that we don't really believe? Does it mean wearing a smiley face on the outside to hide all the negative emotions we feel on the inside? If so, it would be hard to see the benefit. And yet, this is exactly what many of us think. And, why many of us need to reshape our understanding of what it really means to calm down.

According to the Macmillan online dictionary, "Calm down," is a phrasal verb, meaning: "To begin to feel more relaxed and less emotional, or to make someone do this. To make someone less angry. To be, or to become calm and stop worrying."

- Calming yourself down is also referred to as self-soothing.

- Calming down is a form of resilience -- an ability to recover from emotional blows.

- Calming down is a choice. Just as we can magnify our bad emotions by choosing to give them our attention, we can magnify our good emotions by choosing to give them our attention instead.

- Calming down is a re-centering of focus. It means choosing to become aware of the threat within us. Recognizing our negative mental patterns, our shortsightedness, and the consequences they may be creating.

- Calming down is, simply put, a return to normalcy. It means coming back to an inner central place of stability that we often don't even realize we've drifted from, where our hearts and minds are no longer racing, and we can focus, be present, and enjoy life.

- Calming down is a focus on self, rather than on somebody else's mood or behavior. It is about looking at our own actions, not somebody else's. Looking at our own increased heart rates and our own negative thoughts and actions.

- Calming down is for our benefit. Even though it is something that we may only be doing for show, or because somebody told us to do it, it's something that we ourselves are most rewarded by if we actually succeed.

- Calming down is a skill -- something that we can learn and get better at. Something that we can teach ourselves to do whenever our emotions compel us to say or do unproductive things.

FORMING A FOUNDATION

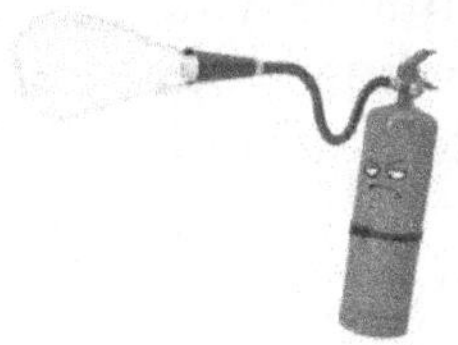

Now, to form a basis for the material that we'll cover in this book, let's go over a few important points.

POINT # 1. IT WILL REQUIRE PREPARATION

It is worth saying again that learning how to calm down is not an easy goal. And, if we are serious about success, we will have to take extra measures. We should know that when the time comes to calm down, we won't be inspired by the same constructive feelings that we are inspired by now. We'll be feeling inspired by totally different feelings – ones that compel us to flee, destroy, or attack.

So, before those trying moments come, we should prepare ourselves as realistically as we can. If we create lists that help remind us of what we really want out of life, that clear view of our goals may help us avoid doing things to sabotage them.

Please try to finish the following lists as honestly and as completely as possible. They will give you some insight into what makes you tick. They will come in helpful later on when your computer freezes up, causing you to lose hours of unsaved work, and you need to remember why it's not a good idea to throw your monitor through the window.

LIST #1: Name five things you will never do, no matter how worked up you get.

I will never:

1. Use derogatory words in an argument (Example).
2. Inflict physical pain on a person I care about (Example).
3.
4.
5.

LIST #2: Decide where your emotional threshold is. This is the point that, when reached, you will devote your full attention to calming down.

I know that it's time to devote my full attention to calming down when:

1. I am contemplating hurting a relationship with somebody that I care about (Example).
2. My frustrations interrupt my ability to focus for more than a half hour (Example).

3.
4.
5.

LIST # 3: Name five things that you are most prone to getting worked up about.

The things that get me most worked up are:

1. When my spouse doesn't understand me (Example).
2. When my kids do things to irritate me intentionally (Example).
3.
4.
5.

LIST # 4: Name 5 reasons you want to get better at calming down.

I want to get better at calming down because:

1. Last year, when my daughter ran away for two days, I realized that my tantrums were jeopardizing my relationships (Example).
2. I want my coworkers to respect me more (Example).
3.
4.
5.

LIST #5: List five of your true goals in life.

My life goals are to:

1. Have strong relationships with every person in my immediate family (Example).
2. Leave a legacy that my friends and family can be proud of (Example).
3.
4.
5.

LIST #6: List five things you care a lot about, which depend on your ability to calm down.

The things I care about that depend on my ability to stay calm, are:

1. My family (Example).
2. My job (Example).
3.
4.
5.

Knowing how you fill in these spaces will put you at the front of the class. You will have a way to stay anchored when you the winds of life tempt you to drift. Please keep these lists handy. Make sure that once you've filled them out, you have them available during crucial moments.

POINT #2. IT WILL HAVE TO BE SOMETHING YOU WANT

Years ago, my family once noticed that Ernie, our dog, had broken a tooth. We didn't know how it had happened. So, we decided to keep an eye on him to see if we could pinpoint the problem.

A short time later, one of us saw him out in the yard, biting the base of the tetherball pole. I went out to try to get him to stop, but he didn't want to let go. He just kept snarling and biting the pole. It was like he couldn't see me or hear me -- as though he had totally tuned the world out. This happened a number of times.

None of us understood why he was so interested in biting the pole -- especially when it was clearly hurting his teeth, and probably even more. We couldn't understand why on earth he was so determined to do something so silly and self-destructive.

Now though, many years later, I think I understand. I think I've even come to see how I am a bit like him. Sometimes, when there's a thought that's hurting me, I too do not want to let go. I grab it with all my might and tune out everything else.

Some part of me may even be aware that what I'm doing is harmful, but that wiser part of me is overpowered by the part of me that enjoys feeling angry and ungoverned. I may do certain things to convince myself that I'm trying to become calmer, but I fail because, in my heart of hearts, I'm not really trying.

When we're worked up, this is quite often the real issue. Though it feels impossible for us to calm down, we probably actually could if we wanted to. Instead, some part of us prefers to latch onto those bad emotions -- just like Ernie, latching onto that pole. We may go through all the right motions, making attempts to calm down that are futile, because we can't really do something against our own will. I believe we make a mistake when we try to force ourselves to calm down, rather than looking at the errors in our logic that are causing us to want to stay worked up.

In a section ahead, called *Misconceptions*, I will talk about our most common logical errors, and explain why they are flawed. Sometimes, this is the quickest way to regaining control of our emotions -- when getting the right result is as simple as wanting it, all we really need is to make ourselves realize ***why*** we want it.

POINT #3. IT'S ABOUT GETTING BACK IN TOUCH

Being worked up makes you less likely to notice what's going on around you — more out of touch with the here and now. You may be out throwing darts with your friends, but you're really just wondering if the check to the landlord will clear. You may be sitting there at your work meeting, but you're really just thinking about that fight you had with your wife this morning.

This is also why your memory is usually foggy in the aftermath of these moments. You can't remember who won at darts. You can't remember what was said at the meeting. You can't even remember what that fight with your wife was about, even though it made you think for a short time that the world was ending. Memories of stressful moments are often lost, because they're moments we weren't really present in.

POINT #4. IT AFFECTS YOUR COMMUNICATION (which affects everything else in your life)

It would only seem logical to say that, as a person's levels of need and urgency increase, his effectiveness as a communicator ought to increase at the same capacity. However, we seem to find the opposite happening; the greater our states of need and urgency, the worse we tend to be at communicating.

Most of us don't know that our communication is broken, because most of the time, the break doesn't affect us. It goes unnoticed, like a crack in a paddle that a boater uses as he paddles on peaceful waters. The only time the paddle breaks, is when the boater enters the rapids, and a lot of pressure is added to it. This also happens to be right when the boater is relying on the paddle more than ever. Haven't you noticed that this is when your communication breaks? Right during the rapids of life?

In low-pressure situations, you have no problems communicating. You're able to tell your barista exactly how you want your coffee, what you'd like in it, and which temperature it should be. You are even able to smile and make eye contact while you do it. But those amazing communication skills seem to disappear when you are under pressure.

When tomorrow is a big holiday and your house is a mess, and your husband and your kids are just sitting on the couch watching TV, it's suddenly harder to make a calm, clear request that accurately conveys your state of need. Instead, you shout. You vent. You say whatever is at the tip of your tongue. You tell your husband and kids to get their lazy butts up and do something useful. You may even use sarcasm and personal attacks to make your expressions more emphatic.

But for some reason, your family doesn't interpret this as a subliminal cry for help. Rather than rushing to your side to rescue you, your husband becomes defensive and storms off. Your kids disperse and hide in their rooms. These people you are counting on so much for help are repelled by you -- right when you need them most. Not because they are unavailable or unwilling, but because ***YOUR*** ability to communicate has diminished to the point of attacking.

This phenomenon seems to stay consistent at all varying levels of need. Even in the most extreme cases, we see poor communication correlating with situational direness. A man who is choking, for example, cannot even speak. His requests for help come out as gasps. His panic is easily misinterpreted and may even create difficulty for those trying to rescue him. Of course, he is not doing this willfully; he is actually physically unable to communicate any better. Doesn't this describe what happens to us when we feel like we are drowning in life?

Some of it is because we aren't able to be ourselves. Our hearts are racing. Our bodies are secreting more adrenaline. Our blood pressure is rising. The blood flow that normally supplies our brains is being diverted to our extremities, preparing us to run from whatever threat that it senses.

Of course, it may not be a real threat, but our instincts don't know that. They treat all threats the same, whether we are trying to run for our lives from a hungry, carnivorous predator, or simply trying to communicate a difficult request to our loved ones.

Simply put, we temporarily trade our IQ points for an adrenaline high. And, in such moments, we'd often be better off taking no action at all until our fear, stress, or anger have passed.

The main thing here is to recognize this strange phenomenon and use it as motivation to work on staying calm. This will make us better equipped for those moments when good communication is most needed (and most difficult). And, it can help us avoid pushing people away when we need their help more than ever.

POINT #5. IT'S ABOUT EMOTIONS

When I started out as a paramedic, I remember being surprised by my psych patients. Not because they were crazy, but because they were so normal. Until then, I had always envisioned them as lunatics. Foaming at the mouth. Trying to chew their way out of straightjackets. I never thought they could be well-educated, charismatic people -- people who even possessed great values. It scared me to see that there were no clear distinctions between them and me.

Yet, over time, I began to recognize that there ***was*** something they were lacking -- not intelligence, but rather, something that kept them grounded to their intelligence. Something that kept them from betraying their intelligence when the pressures of life stacked up. You might say that what they lacked was "Emotional intelligence."

Dan Goleman introduced this concept in his book, Emotional Intelligence. He describes it as the ability to live without being controlled by emotion and believes that it is often even more critical to a person's success than his IQ.

Many of us lack emotional intelligence simply because we don't see its value. Probably, because emotions don't seem like a major component in most of our problems. Money issues. Housework. Things that break and need fixing. Most of this seems purely practical in nature.

When we're driving down the road and the car engine dies, we never see it as an emotional problem. And yet, hindsight has shown us that such situations are quite emotionally taxing. And, if we don't stop and address how our emotions are affecting us, we often end up with even bigger problems -- ones that make our original problem seem tiny in comparison.

Not to say that the practical portion of the problem isn't important, because it is. It involves doing something about our problems. The thing is, we are usually much better at it if our minds are clear first.

So, next time you're worked up, try to spot how it is affecting your emotions. Try to focus on becoming calm before making decisions or taking actions. That is, if your situation allows you to.

Solve the emotional half of the problem first. Then solve the other half of the problem. If you think you can't afford to stop and get your emotions back in check, think again. You probably can't afford ***not*** to.

SHORT STORY #1. THE LONG DRIVE

A few years back, I worked with a guy named Xavier. One day, while we were working, a message was sent to our pagers, which said, "Come to headquarters now."

We weren't sure why we were being called to headquarters, but we were nervous about it. It usually wasn't a good omen. It rarely ever meant that you were getting a raise or a promotion. It often meant that you had done something wrong, and it was now going to be dealt with punitively.

When we arrived at headquarters, two managers greeted us. They immediately split us up. First, they pulled me into a room and told me about a few complaints that had recently been made about Xavier. When they were done talking to me, they called Xavier into the room to get his side of the story.

I sat outside and waited. I couldn't hear what they were saying, but the room had windows, so I could see what was going on. Xavier was defending himself against some complaints that had been made against him.

I could see he was getting worked up as he talked. His face was turning red. He was becoming animated. He was flailing his arms and raising his voice. Occasionally, I could hear the loud, muffled tones of his voice, escaping through the wall. While he may have been speaking in his own defense, it was clearly only hurting his case; not helping it.

At the end of the meeting, they told Xavier to leave his pager and his ID card behind. They had decided to put him on a twenty-four-hour suspension while they thought about how they would proceed. In the meantime, he was told not to call or text or email anyone in the company. This was to be a time of "cooling down," so to speak.

But the next morning when I came in, I was told that Xavier had been let go. I was surprised. Not just because I thought they were going to give him a second chance, but because his dismissal didn't have anything to do with the complaints that had been made against him. They fired him because of how he had acted during his cool-down period.

During that time, he texted, emailed, and called nearly every manager in the company -- pleading with them, begging them to consider his innocence, and restating his case over and over. This was ***exactly*** what they told him not to do.

He had gotten so worked up that he just couldn't sit still and keep his phone in his pocket for 24 hours, even when that was all he needed to do to keep his job. It was confirmed for me by a valid source that they never actually planned on firing him. They only fired him because of how poorly he handled the confrontation.

It's interesting to me that what brought him down wasn't any real threat at all, but rather, the way he acted when he thought a threat was present. It shows that sometimes our problems are more than just partially emotional; sometimes, they are purely emotional. Sometimes, the only real threat is one we create by acting irrationally.

If only we learned to make calming down a priority. We would see that a lot of the threats we fear aren't even real. And, we would avoid handling our situations in ways that create real problems. Sometimes, the best thing to do is nothing. Just calm down and recognize that our impulses to act would only be creating problems where there are none.

POINT # 6. IT'S ABOUT GETTING BACK IN YOUR LIFE'S DRIVER'S SEAT

In a big way, calming down is about learning to take back control over your life. It's about learning to be in charge of your own emotions and decisions once again.

In the field of psychology, the term, "Locus of control," refers to the extent that people are able to govern the events that influence their lives. A person's "Locus of control" is considered to be a direct determiner of the amount of happiness that he/she feels.

Generally, a person who feels stuck -- financially, emotionally, or relationally -- isn't as happy as someone who feels in control in those areas. It may sound like an oversimplification, but it's not. A good amount of research backs it up.

If you don't feel happy, control may just be what you need. And, don't worry -- we're not talking about the bad kind of control -- the kind that dictators and abusive spouses use, but the good kind of control -- the kind that gives you freedom over your own life -- to do, say, and be as you wish.

It's the kind of control that the Bible speaks of, when it says, "It is better to win control over yourself than over whole cities." Doesn't that sound like a good kind of control? Doesn't it sound like exactly what your life needs?

The good news is that nothing is holding you back. To gain control over your life again, the only thing required is that you reach out and take it. That, and one other small thing -- you have to stop blaming. If you are a person who blames, then this is a critical first step for you.

BLAME

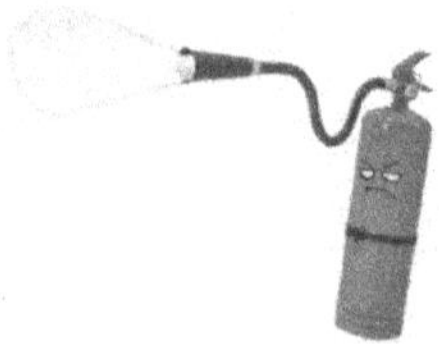

In the show, "The Dog Whisperer," a known dog expert named Cesar Milan goes into homes to help people out whose dogs are out of control. And, he is usually pretty good at diagnosing the problem -- not so much in the dogs, but in their owners.

He shows them that they are responsible for the ways their pets are misbehaving. They are bringing the bad energy into their interactions with their dogs which their dogs are only responding to. Of course, this comes as quite a surprise to many people -- especially when it seems clear that the dogs are the ones causing the problem. Cesar shows them otherwise. As he often says, "I rehabilitate dogs. I train people."

Many of us are a lot like these dog owners in the way that we don't see how we are contributing to our problems. We need training. We spot the problem everywhere but in ourselves. We think that whatever is causing us stress is the issue. A sibling or a spouse. A circumstance. A person who we are having difficulty dealing with.

We blame traffic jams and spilled glasses of milk for our overreactions, but these things aren't to blame. They only expose how prone we are to over-reacting.

We often blame tough conversational subjects, such as money, politics, or parenting, simply because these things get us worked up just thinking about them. But again, the real problem has nothing to do with them. The real problem is somewhere in us. It's in our responses to these things.

When we blame, we make our problems worse than they have to be. One reason is because other people are provoked by our blaming. They don't like being blamed. They don't like being seen as the problem. And, they usually have a very keen sense for when somebody is trying to blame them. They detect it in even the subtlest of gestures and are immediately put on defense.

When we wag our fingers at them. When we give them a contemptuous look. When we are short with them, roll our eyes at them, or act righteously indignant toward them. Or, heaven forbid, when we shush them.

These are all things we are far more likely to do when we're seeing somebody else as the problem, simply because our excitement is like a heavy weight we are trying to shrug off onto whatever or whomever we can in order to make our own loads lighter.

Most of us don't do this intentionally; we do it instinctively, or out of habit. It is a pattern that has long been ingrained into us, and we've never properly dealt with it. Perhaps, because we thought it would go away all on its own.

We thought we'd automatically be calmer once we were past the pressures of high school. Once we were graduated from college. Once we owned a house, got married, and had kids. Obviously, those things didn't make us calmer. If there's one thing that's proven true, it's that we never really reach a lush plateau where things suddenly stop getting the better of us.

No matter how much time we're given, we still end up being stressed at the very last minute. No matter how positive a situation's outcome, we still end up fretting and worrying until we know how it plays out. No matter how great our relationships may be, we still always find things about them that bring us to the point of acting irrational and neurotic.

The only thing that's changing about our stress is the face that it wears. Our reactions to it bear a striking similarity throughout all of life's seasons. It all just goes to show that we've got it wrong; it's not the stress of life that needs fixing; it's our way of relating to it. It's the way we carry our load that is far more important than the load's type, weight, or size. This stays true whether we're nine years old and stressing out over a mean kid who won't share the slide with us, or seventy-five years old and worried about this month's social security check.

Despite all that we've been through, our problem is that we aren't developing better strategies for dealing with our stress -- ones that don't toss out our peace and clarity. We are the common denominator in all of our worked-up moments. This may be the single most valuable lesson that our frustrations have to teach us.

Our blame says more about us than it does about anything else. It reveals our own biases, attitudes, and patterns, as well as the ease with which we overlook our internal faults to find fault externally. It reveals a lot about ***when*** we are prone to blaming, as well as ***which*** types of things we blame.

Do you have blaming tendencies? If so, it probably means that you aren't prone to seeing your problems as your own. When you walk away from a bad argument with your husband, you think ***he's*** the difficult person. ***He's*** the one who can't be reasoned with. ***He's*** the source of the problem; not you.

It's not that you're too sensitive; it's that he's too insensitive. It's not that you're too defensive; it's that he's too offensive. It's not that you're bad at communicating; it's that he's a bad listener, and so on. Every failed interaction seems to point blame at something other than you.

The main concern with these biases is that they decrease your chances of finding good solutions, because you're only interested in ones that align with your self-presumed innocence -- ones that make him look crazy and you look sane. You rule out propositions that would actually deal with the problem you're most affected by -- the one inside yourself.

Tell me... how do you look at the disasters that litter your past? Do you look past your own faults in them? Do you see them as minor, or as somebody else's? Do you think they are the product of somebody pushing you too far, as though your response wasn't really your responsibility? If so, that is the absolute wrong perspective.

No doubt, your husband may have done or said some pretty mean things to you, which have made it easy for you to say and do some hurtful things back. But you alone are at fault for every improper thing you've ever done and said. No one was putting a gun to your head. If you are willing to dismiss your own faults so easily, you should be just as quick to dismiss the faults of those who have wronged you.

It's not easy to let go of blame -- especially when you know that you truly have been wronged. Especially when it seems that your part in the problem was so much smaller than somebody else's. Especially when you've been treated unfairly, and have had to deal with a lot that was just plain sad.

But, do you want to know what would be even sadder? If you concluded that it all was somebody else's problem. If you decided that your own life quality depended on somebody else changing. That, my friend, would be the saddest thing of all.

Taking control of your life, at least in a large part, is about learning how to stop blaming. Learning to let go of those well-thought-out excuses that you keep at the tip of your tongue that make you look like the good guy in your friends' eyes. Your family's eyes.

Your own eyes. As long as you're clinging to those excuses, you are giving your control away. And, your happiness.

The choice comes down to two things: a good excuse, or a good life. Whichever of these you choose usually comes at the expense of the other. If you really want a better life, it will cost you your excuse. If you just want to keep your excuse, you can bypass all of that uncomfortable inward reflection stuff. It doesn't matter how good or bad your excuse is. Any excuse will spare you from the hard work of change that rarely sounds fun to most of us.

Few of us make this choice knowingly. We make it instinctively, leaning toward whichever path it is that offers the least resistance. It's easier to think of others as the problem, rather than ourselves. It's easier to notice a room full of crazy people, rather than how they may only be acting crazy because of something ***we*** are doing. It's easy for us to be like these dog owners who don't see how their own negative energy is inviting the bad reactions they despise in their dogs. If our faults play any role at all, we need to be extremely careful not to minimize it.

If you want a more peaceful environment, then ***you*** have to be the one to set the tone. That is the only way this will work. You can't get just as crazy as your kids when they start shouting and crying in the supermarket aisles. You can't flip out at your husband when he flips out at you. You can't stay focused on the craziness of others, using it as an excuse to justify your own bad reactions. You can't keep telling people that they need to relax, when you need to relax just as badly (if not more). Not only is that ineffective; it's hypocritical.

You need to focus on the one thing that you actually have some power to change -- yourself. It's hard, but it's the only real key to freedom. Own your responses. Own your overreactions. They're ***your*** problem; not someone else's. They pose more of a threat to your well-being than they do to any other person on this planet.

Don't worry -- if you take this brave step, it doesn't mean that you are letting others off the hook for their unfair or unkind treatment of you. It just means you're choosing a healthier way of responding -- one that doesn't cost you your own freedom, happiness, and peace of mind.

Here is a test to see if you are a blamer. Answer yes or no to the following ten questions.

THE BLAMER'S TEST

1. *Do you commonly feel like a victim?*
2. *Do you commonly feel unhappy due to uncontrollable circumstances?*
3. *Do you ever feel that your response is someone else's responsibility?*
4. *Do your past overreactions cause you to think of somebody other than yourself?*
5. *When you're frustrated, do you see it as a sign that someone else must have done something to make you feel that way?*
6. *When something goes wrong, do you instantly start forming a case to prove your innocence?*
7. *Do you tend to think more about* ***who*** *caused a problem than* ***what*** *needs to be done to solve it?*
8. *Do you have a hard time saying you're sorry?*
9. *Do you ever feel that admitting your own mistakes would let other people off the hook for their mistakes?*
10. *Do you commonly feel that your life would be better if only the people around you were smarter, quicker, or more responsible?*

If you answered yes to three or more of these questions, there is an increasingly good chance that you are a blamer. And, a good chance that your blaming tendencies are keeping you from being in the driver's seat of your life.

Of course, this test is subjective. It is basically just a tool to get you to look at yourself in a new way and see if you notice any hidden tendencies. Ultimately, learning how to stop blaming will make you better at calming down, which, after all, is the whole goal of this book.

If you have discovered that you have some blaming tendencies, and would like to know how to change them, here are three ways you can start:

1. Work on being happy.

Before you ever allow yourself to blame anyone again, make a deal with yourself that you will first make it a goal to focus on being happy. Why will this help? Because, as long as you think that your happiness depends on someone or something else, you have already failed the prerequisite to being happy, which is: being responsible for your own happiness. That is why this is such a good starting point. Work on your own happiness. Once you have achieved that, you may then proceed to the next step, which is: assigning blame. If you do this in the right order, you probably won't feel the need to assign any blame, because you'll no longer be looking for an excuse to pin your unhappiness on. If, by some chance, you still feel the need to assign blame, you will at least know that you aren't doing it simply to find a convenient scapegoat. Working on your own happiness is a win/win situation. First, it keeps you from being miserable. Second, it keeps you from making silly excuses just to justify that misery.

2. Work on being more lenient.

If you are someone who commonly gets worked up, it may be because you aren't lenient enough. Rather than noticing a world full of things that are upsetting, you'd be better off learning to adapt to your world. Rather than seeing your wife's undecipherable looks as mean or critical, simply teach yourself that her expressions aren't a big deal. Teach yourself to be more adaptable and flexible by increasing your threshold for small discomforts and annoyances. Learn how to be more lenient, and you'll soon find the world less full of things that you find fault with.

3. Work on being more positive.

Have you ever noticed that when you buy a car, you suddenly begin to notice every other car on the road like it? You never knew how many burgundy Toyota Siennas were on the road. But, now that you own one, you notice every single one. Something similar is true about the traits we possess. We tend to notice our own traits in others. Defensive people notice the defensive trait in others. Critical people notice the critical trait in others. Proud people are quick to notice when others are displaying pride, and blamers are quickest to notice when other people are blaming. So, if you look down the highway of life and see nothing but blamers, what does this say about you? Maybe, it's time to give your perspective a tune-up. Start being the first to notice the good. Be the first to pay people compliments for even their small efforts. Be the first to own your share of the blame. You will soon see fewer blamers on the road, and you will be less of a blamer yourself.

OTHER BARRIERS

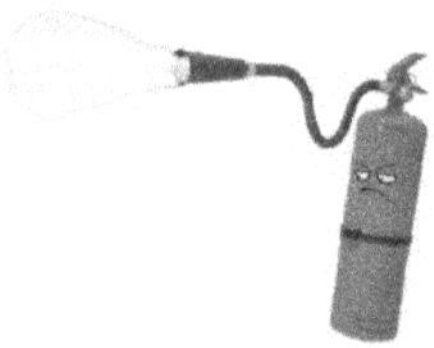

So, now that we've talked a fair deal about the significance of blame and how it relates to our ability to calm down, we should talk about some of the other major barriers that commonly stand in our way.

Here are the most common barriers we face.

PROCRASTINATION

We wait too long to do or say something about a developing problem. By the time we get around to taking action, it is only because it has escalated in severity and is no longer ignorable.

While we often think our problems are the result of having too little time, they are more often the result of mismanaged time.

Many of our problems wouldn't even be problems, if only we were better at confronting them sooner.

CAMOUFLAGE

We fail even to notice that we are getting excited. Our excitedness somehow gets camouflaged in with everything else that's going on. Since we don't see it, we don't stop to address it.

DOWNPLAYING

This is when we DO see our excitedness, but downplay its importance, because of its smallness in comparison to our other problems. We feel like we've got bigger fish to fry, so our out-of-control emotional state takes a backseat.

MOMENTUM

Momentum is the force that keeps things going in whichever direction they are already headed in. It seems to be affected by many things. It is affected by our habits; as we too are likely to keep behaving in ways we are already accustomed to behaving in. It even seems to share its effects between individuals, as people seem to adopt each other's dispositions.

It's one reason why you see mass panic during disasters. One person starts panicking simply because he sees his neighbor panicking. It's also why you sometimes find yourself in a bad mood when your spouse is in a bad mood. This almost-contagious effect of momentum makes it an especially difficult barrier to overcome. Once one person in a group starts losing control, the rest in the group become even more likely to follow.

BLIND SPOTS

This is when we can't really see ourselves or our situations objectively. It's when we fail to recognize that we are getting upset, or we fail to understand what is making us upset. It may be clear to others who are observing us, but unclear to us.

Our blind spots seem to hurt us most when we are worked up. They make us less prone to seeing the problem we are facing, and thus, make it increasingly harder to solve. Blind spots are a difficult barrier to overcome, simply because we cannot count on our own senses to spot them.

DISCOURAGEMENT

We feel helpless about our emotions. We feel like it's too late to stop them. The damage has been done, and there is no longer any point in trying to practice restraint.

Or, we feel like we've already tried everything before and none of it has worked. So, what's the point in trying again? Especially when so many times it has only made things worse instead of better.

THRILL

We enjoy the feeling of being worked up. The sense of power it gives us. The sense of certainty that it adorns us with against otherwise frightening unknowns. It all gives us a type of high that we may not want to come down from.

PRIDE

Our egos convince us that we are above the problem. Or, that there is something wrong with us if we give too much care or thought to our emotions. Pride keeps us from desiring real progress and chasing the appearance of progress instead.

We may choose not to want positive changes simply because they would prove that we were causing the problem. Pride keeps us more interested in avoiding blame and negative stigmatizations than in finding actual solutions.

MIS-PRIORITIZATION

This is when we place other virtues in front of the virtue of staying calm. Being productive. Being on time. Being heard. Being right. Being tidy. Our number one goal is to make sure that the house is spotless, that the kids get to soccer on time, and that everyone looks immaculate for family pictures. But, none of that matters.

Not if, in the process, we injure relationships, damage our reputations, and create hysteria in the people around us. Whatever good we managed to accomplish gets overshadowed by the damage that was done by our craziness.

SELF-DECEPTION

Self-deception is another common obstacle. When you are mad at your wife, you don't want to consider that her point of view may have some validity. When you are upset at life, you don't want to think about how you may be partially responsible for how poorly it's going. You form a resistance to certain parts of the truth. Unfortunately, these are often the same parts that would put you back in touch with your sanity.

Why on earth would you wander from your sanity? Because your misery somehow seems lessened by believing that you were right and someone else was wrong, or that your contribution to the chaos wasn't quite as significant as somebody else's. When nothing else seems to be going right, you might as well latch onto a narrative that at least lets you feel decent about yourself.

Of course, you usually don't do this intentionally either. It's not that you are interested in believing lies, but that you are invested in yourself, and in perspectives that keep you seeing the best in yourself. Unfortunately, you are capable of doing this at the cost of truth and objectivity.

TIMING

In our clear moments, we typically have purer desires. We want what's best for ourselves -- to become calmer, saner, and more patient people. But, when we are worked up, we have other desires. We want to stay worked up.

We want to fester in our bad emotions and throw caution to the wind. Sadly, our good desires get lost right when they would have their greatest chance to do us some good. The problem isn't a matter of desire, but of timing. We want the right thing; just not at the right time.

MISCONCEPTIONS

During these moments when we lose our good desires, it is usually due to errors in our thinking. We might call these thought errors "misconceptions." They are the barriers that exist in our minds. And, they are the easiest type of barrier to overcome -- when the problem is in our heads, the solution is too. All we have to do is change the way we think!

If a man is bothered by the sound of the rain on his rooftop, he need not learn how to stop the rain. He need only learn how to change the way he feels about the rain, which is a far simpler feat than trying to learn to control the weather. Most of us do not need to make huge changes to our worlds; we just need to find and change what is causing us not to see our worlds in a good light.

In the following section, we'll look deeper at some of these common false perspectives that we have and explore what makes them flawed. If you find yourself occasionally having these false perspectives, you are in luck. It means that your calmness doesn't depend on making huge life changes. It just depends on making simple changes in how you think.

MISCONCEPTIONS

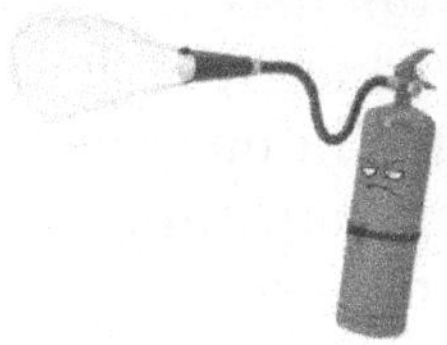

MY EXCITEDNESS PROVES THAT I CARE

Under this misconception, we assume that there is a link between how much a person cares and how excited he gets. For example, a man who shows no emotion seems not to care very much about his problem. Yet, if he appears to be worked up, he somehow looks less apathetic.

Remember last year when everyone in your family was reacting to the President's new tax plan? You forced a reaction too, simply because you knew you would look like a stoic boob if you didn't.

The problem is that real concern isn't always visible. Some caring people aren't expressive at all. Some uncaring people are expressive about everything. You simply cannot always tell by looking, and you risk creating new problems if you get worked up in order to prove you care.

I GET MORE DONE WHEN I'M WORKED UP

This is when we think that we have to get worked up in order to be productive. Why do we think this? Because, many times in our lives, it has been true -- we didn't get up off our bums until we were finally upset enough to do something about our problem. Now, a link forever exists in our minds between getting worked up and getting things done.

Of course, this is a fallacy. Intense emotion is an unnecessary (and often destructive) additive to productivity. In fact, many of us get worked up ***instead*** of becoming productive. Being worked up makes us feel like we are doing something about our problem, when really, we may not be. The only demonstrable thing we are changing is our emotions.

I'M A SHARPER THINKER WHEN I'M WORKED UP

This is when we think that our level of mental competence increases with our excitedness. It's why many of us turn into maniacs right when we have a tough job to do. The thing is, we would actually think more clearly if we were able to operate calmly. We'd be less distracted. More aware of diversions that cause us to stray from our real goals.

The best athletes, the best marriage partners, and the best business negotiators seem to know this, and all seem to have this single trait in common -- the ability stay calm amidst emotional pressures. They maintain a calm disposition even when the stakes are high and when everyone else is overreacting. Staying calm is what makes them great at what they do.

I'M MORE PERSUASIVE WHEN I'M WORKED UP

In the game of poker, a player will often raise the bet. When he does this, it usually indicates one of two things -- either that he has really good cards, or that he wants you to ***THINK*** he has really good cards.

Regardless of the cards he is actually holding, this bold move has an intimidating effect on his opponents, causing some of them to back down. This is precisely the goal.

Often, we attempt the same thing in our communication. Rather than simply saying what we want to say, we “raise the bet,” so to speak. We deliver our message with dramatic tones and inflections, hoping that our intenseness adds perceived value to what we are saying.

The funny thing is that this often has the opposite effect than the one we desired. People see our dramatization as a sign that our message lacks value. If it didn't, we would not feel the need to dress it up with dramatization.

PEOPLE ONLY LISTEN TO ME WHEN I’M WORKED UP

This is when you use excitedness to spark a sense of urgency in others. Rather than telling your wife calmly that you don’t like how she’s driving, you lose your cool. You freak out, hoping that she’ll sense the importance of your message without you having to use proper communication.

It seems effective, because it now suddenly feels like she’s giving you her full attention. But, she’s not. She is only stunned. She isn’t hearing your words; she’s only noticing your abrasiveness, your aggression, and your loudness. She's not paying any attention to your message, because she's too distracted by the crazy messenger.

It may very well seem that she doesn't hear you when you use your calm voice, but if that's true, it's an entirely different problem. It won't ever get solved by drawing attention to how loud and frantic you can be. What you need is a solution; not more problems. Stop getting worked up, believing that it makes people listen. It doesn't. It just guarantees that something other than your message will be the point of focus.

I HAVE MORE CONTROL OVER THINGS WHEN I'M WORKED UP

I think we would all agree that fear and sadness are hard emotions to handle. They often make us feel like we have no control. This is why many of us, whenever we are confronted by these tough emotions, become angry instead. Anger lets us feel like there is some part of our situation that we ***are*** in charge of.

The truth, however, is that being angry doesn't actually give us control. In fact, it often only gives us one more negative emotion amidst the other negative emotions we are already feeling. Now, not only do we have the fear or sadness we were originally dealing with, we have anger to deal with too.

I STAY PROTECTED BY GETTING WORKED UP

Perhaps you've noticed that many of us get angry when we feel intimidated, or when our own point of view is being threatened. Out of defense, we stomp. We shout. We puff out our chests. We hope to scare the threat away by making our presence seem bigger. But it usually doesn't have that effect. In fact, it often has the opposite effect.

Our excitement tends to be perceived as weakness, not strength. Others see it as a sign that we have lost control, and that they have a chance to take it. We play into the hands of the bullies and opportunists of the world who are only out to do us harm.

We would actually demonstrate a lot more strength by showing that we can stay ***calm*** in the face of provocation. Others would see that we are mentally and emotionally resilient, and that they don't have the power to sway us.

I AM BETTER AT FACING THE UNKNOWN WHEN I'M WORKED UP

This is when we assume that being worked up makes us ready for anything. We fear an impact coming, and we psych ourselves up to face it. We brace ourselves for whatever comes our way. Again, this often has the opposite effect than the one we desire.

In a car crash, an intoxicated person usually suffers less harm than the sober person who sees the crash coming and has time to brace for it. A similar effect is true when it comes to emotional excitedness. We tend to handle life's impacts better when we meet them with a calmer mind.

MY EXCITEDNESS PROVES THAT I HAVE A BRAIN

A person's outward expressions can't always tell us what is going on inside him. And yet, this doesn't stop most of us from trying to judge a book by its cover. One thing we try to determine by external signs is a person's level of intelligence.

We tend to think a person is just a little bit smarter if he is worked up about his problem. He creates the impression that he grasps the magnitude of his situation and that he is doing something about it. If you saw a man in a burning building who looked a little too calm, it would be easy to assume that he wasn't quite as smart as those other people, panicking and scrambling for the exits.

However, this is a flawed way of assessing a person's intelligence. After all, there are plenty of people who don't show much expression at all -- even when they are facing intimidating giants. Even when they have a laser focus and are working to solve the problem internally. It seems that an overreaction is really only proof of one thing -- that a person responds to stress by throwing some of his control away, which actually, isn't very smart at all.

IT'S OKAY TO GET WORKED UP WHEN SOMEBODY GIVES ME THE RIGHT

This is when we assume that our upsetness is okay... maybe even necessary for serving justice. Your spouse made you angry. He goofed up so badly that he doesn't deserve the calm you. He deserves the angry, rigid, shouting you. It's okay if you're worked up. You clearly have the right to be!

So, you serve justice by losing your cool. You yell, shout, and forfeit all restraint. But, does this accomplish anything? No. At least, not anything good. Now, you're both acting stupid, rather than just one of you. You are both being punished for the one person's crime.

When you get worked up in response to someone else's stupidity, it's like slapping yourself in the face and hoping they feel it. Since when has it been good revenge to share punishment with the offender?

Since when has justice been served by throwing your own credibility and peace of mind out the window?

The worst way you punish yourself is by missing out on the opportunity to communicate. You lose the chance to share your true thoughts, feelings, and desires to somebody you care about, and whom ***you*** would benefit by expressing yourself to. Wouldn't that be a more worthwhile outcome? Lesson: it doesn't help to get worked up just because you ***can***. Having the right to do something doesn't make it smart.

IT'S OKAY IF I'M WORKED UP. MY SITUATION CREATES AN EXCEPTION

While many of us believe that it's not normally smart to get worked up, we commonly give ourselves a hall pass due to the severity or the timing of our problems. And, we tend not to see how many exceptions we are making. It can easily become more common for us to make exceptions to the rules than to obey them.

When you look closely at our situations, it becomes clear that most of our exceptions aren't really justifiable. They just allow us to avoid upholding standards that we want to claim to live by, but find difficult to uphold.

SUMMARY

The main thing to walk away with in all this is that, even though we often have reasons for being worked up, it rarely ever helps us. To summarize this point a, I have created a short list of things that people never say. Here it is:

TEN THINGS PEOPLE NEVER, EVER SAY

1. Bill, this is a large project. We need competent individuals. Find me some people who get worked up about everything. I need some real spazzes!
2. Listen Tom, your offer seems solid. But you didn't freak out once during your presentation! We're sorry... the deal is off.
3. I'm so glad that mom and dad flip out and argue whenever there is a special occasion. I can tell they really want to create good memories for us.
4. Hey, look... mom's in one of her crazy moods. Let's go help her!
5. Thanks for flipping out at me, man. I think that's what made me come around to your way of thinking.
6. Wow bro... I wasn't sure if you had that situation under control, but then I saw you freaking out and couldn't believe I ever doubted you!

7. Great job, Steve. The team appreciates how much you freaked out yesterday. It made the workload lighter for everyone.
8. Sweetheart, I don't understand what you're trying to tell me. Maybe, if you just freaked out a little, I'd understand.
9. The reason I pulled you over, son, was because you were driving too calmly. I'm going to have to write you a citation for failing to wig out.
10. Your honor, thanks for the innocent verdict. I'm glad that despite my lack of evidence, you found my tantrums compelling.

Hopefully, you found these statements humorous, because they were meant to be. I hope you also agree that being worked up doesn't make you more efficient, more proactive, or more intelligent; it makes you more sporadic, less effective, and less prepared.

Let's now move on to the next section, where we will attempt to unravel our misconceptions and explore some of their origins.

A DEEPER LOOK

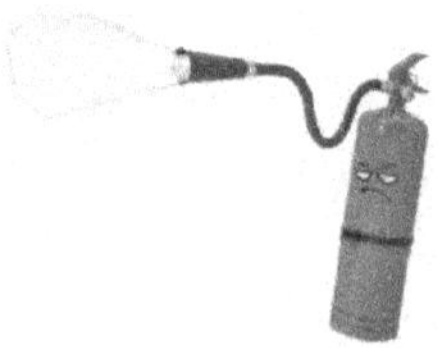

In third grade, I sat next to a boy named Timmy. He was a nice guy, but he got worked up really easily. One day during class, he dropped his pencil. The teacher turned around as he got out of his chair to pick it up. At that point, somebody shouted, “Hey look, Timmy’s out of his seat.”

Everyone looked over at Timmy to see how he would respond. That’s when he exploded into tears in front of everyone, crying and defending himself, explaining that he had only gotten out of his chair to pick up his pencil.

Timmy’s strong reaction surprised us all. And, it showed some of the kids that they now had an easy way to be amused. It soon became a trend to tease Timmy this way whenever the teacher wasn't looking. Every time, it worked as expected. Timmy would always break down into tears and defend himself.

One time, the teacher left the room, and a large group of kids began chanting, "Timmy's out of his seat, Timmy's out of his seat." Timmy's face turned bright red and he started crying and shouting, "I'm not out of my seat. I'm not out of my seat! Stop saying that! It's not true!"

After many years of reflection, I've come to a few important realizations about this experience. One, that some people want us to get upset. That is their main goal. When we lose our cool, we are giving them exactly what they want. I've also learned that the solution is not to try to avoid such people, or to live in some sort of safe space that is free of anyone or anything we find bothersome.

Because, even if we could create a safer world to live in, it would not fix the part of us that is wounded or fragile -- the part that makes us prone to overreacting. The part that makes us sitting ducks whenever new problems surface. This is the part that has to be dealt with if we want more than *surfacy* solutions. It's what is behind our unusual reactions to certain life situations.

In the past, you've noticed that your friend, Bob, doesn't seem to care at all when his wife criticizes his driving. You, however, have trouble staying calm in the same situation. When your wife tells you to slow down, you instantly become unsettled. You internalize and you become rigid. Like Timmy, you need to find out why your reaction is so much stronger when it comes to certain stressors.

If you are daring enough to explore this, you may find your reactions link to certain experiences from your past. Where do your strong reactions come from? Have you ever thought about this?

Remember that time when you lost your parents in the grocery store? It only lasted 10 minutes, but it felt like an eternity. In that short time, you were petrified, wondering if you'd ever see them again. What if a little recollection could help you understand your tendencies and overcome them?

In a book, I read not long ago, called "The DNA of Relationships," author Gary Smalley talks about how most of our overreactions are the result of certain fears. And, he gives a list of what some of those common fears are. They include (but are not limited to):

Fear of pain
Fear of embarrassment

Fear of rejection
Fear of abandonment
Fear of failure
Fear of being helpless
Fear of inadequacy
Fear of being unloved
Fear of being defective
Fear of being worthless
Fear of not measuring up
Fear of being seen as unimportant

Do you recognize any of these fears in you? Perhaps it would be good to remember the immortal words of Franklin D. Roosevelt, stating that "The only thing to fear is fear itself." It's true that our fear often poses a threat greater than any of the things we are afraid of.

Your fear may be the biggest threat you face in life. It could be greater than your check engine light. Greater than your team losing the game. Greater than that jerk who fouled you during your layup and never came clean about it.

Your fear is most likely an even bigger threat to your well-being and peace of mind than any of these things. But, it's a harder threat to spot, because it's not as obvious. It doesn't have horns or a pitchfork tail. It doesn't necessitate immediate intervention. It sits calmly and inconspicuously right inside you, like a wolf dressed as a sheep. There, it gains access to your control panels, making you susceptible to responding poorly to all that happens to you in life.

If you haven't spent much time exploring your own triggers and fears, or if you aren't sure where to start, you may want to look at the usual suspects, such as exhaustion, dehydration, or hunger. A helpful acronym for remembering these is "HALT," which stands for: hungry, angry, lonely, tired. Whenever these conditions are present, you are more susceptible to overreacting.

WHAT I'VE LEARNED

As I mentioned earlier on, my old dog, Ernie, used to bite a rusty pole and damage his teeth. And, I talked about how I am similar. Sometimes, I don't want to let go of the thoughts and feelings that are hurting me. I could calm down, but I don't want to. But I've also realized that when this is happening, I'm rarely aware of it.

Truth be told, I am convinced of the opposite -- I think I want to become calmer and I think I am doing all I can about it. It's not true, of course. The truth is that some small part of me is enjoying being worked up. Some part of me likes how it feels to act on impulses -- to slam doors and make careless comments without any concern to the repercussions.

During these moments, my excitedness is like a drug. It makes me feel like the incredible hulk, rather than just a normal guy. Of course, I fail to notice that my oversized attitude and ego aren't doing me any favors. And, I fail to see that staying this way is optional. I really could snap out of it if I wanted to. But, I don't. That somehow seems unappealing. I don’t really want to turn back into the calmer, more rational me.

Perhaps it is pride that keeps me from recognizing the danger of where I am, like an addict who doesn't want to see that he's fallen off the wagon. Whatever the case, the problem is different than what I think, and therefore, the solution is too.

The issue isn't that none of the solutions work, but that none of them interest me. Therefore, my real need is not to find better solutions, but to become interested in the ones available to me. Getting myself to recognize the futility and destructiveness of staying worked up. Getting myself to see that I am believing certain lies, and to realize how these lies are hurting me. This is my true priority in these moments.

This realization has shown me something very interesting about calming down. In short, I’ve learned that there really are only three reasons why a person would ever fail to calm down. They are:

1. An inability to calm down (which happens but is rare).
2. A lack of will to calm down (which is common).
3. The use of ineffective techniques to calm down (which is also pretty common).

Anytime my emotional engine seems stuck on high idle, it is for one of these three reasons. And, I need not look any further than this when I am troubleshooting the problem.

Only once we understand ***why*** we are worked up, can we begin to see what will help us calm down. Let's look at these three main reasons a little closer. They are the simplest, quickest way to help us find what needs fixing.

REASON #1 - AN INABILITY TO CALM DOWN

There truly are times in life when it is beyond our control to calm down. However, they are rarer than we think. Such experiences may include:

- Drowning
- Suffocating
- Being electrocuted
- Suffering a seizure
- Being attacked by a pack of wolves

- Being in a street fight with Jean Claude Van Damme
- Being held up at gunpoint by Dirty Harry
- All of these things happening at once

During such events, we may actually be physically and mentally incapable of calming down, due to the severity of the situation we're in. For example, if you're choking on a large piece of unchewed meat, it's kind of hard to articulate exactly what you're feeling and what you need.

A different need takes priority over the need to calm down. That is: to escape imminent danger. To get out of harm's way from whatever is threatening your health, your life, your loved ones' lives, or some other thing that you value.

WHAT TO DO IF THIS DESCRIBES YOUR SITUATION

If this describes the situation you are currently in, then please... put this book down and remove yourself from harm's way. Then, once you are no longer defending your home from zombies, trying to keep your car from rolling off a cliff, or trying to outswim an angry alligator, you can continue.

Remember... these highly crucial situations are rarer than we think. We are far more likely to *think* we are in one than actually be in one. It lets us believe that our lost control points to our circumstances, rather than to us.

REASON #2. - A LACK OF WILL TO CALM DOWN

This includes those times when we don't realize that we need to calm down, or don't think of it as being an important need. It includes times when we like the feeling of being worked up or think that our excitedness is doing something favorable for us.

I will talk a little more about this issue shortly, in the section called "*Starting with desire.*" There, I address the significance of the issue, and offer some tips that you may find helpful.

WHAT TO DO IF THIS DESCRIBES YOUR SITUATION

A. Go back and read the *Misconceptions* section. Find the misconception that is affecting your thinking and correct it. Or, you should:

B. Focus on some kind of physical exercise. While you may not be able to ***force*** yourself to feel calm, you ***can*** force yourself to do things that will inadvertently make you feel calmer. Find a physical exercise from the "*Stuff that works*" section and apply it to have a direct effect on the way you feel.

REASON #3. - USING INEFFECTIVE TECHNIQUES TO CALM DOWN

This is when we realize the need to become calm, we want to become calm, and we actually try to become calm, but, for whatever reason, we fail. Maybe, we don't give enough effort. Maybe, we don't try for a long enough period of time. Or, maybe the effort we give is spent on techniques that are ineffective.

WHAT TO DO IF THIS DESCRIBES YOUR SITUATION

If this describes your situation, it may help you to read through the following list, which displays the most common failed techniques we use attempting to become calmer.

THE STUFF THAT DOESN'T WORK

SAYING "CALM DOWN"

This is when we think that calmness can be commanded. Someone is worked up, and we say, "Calm down." Not only are we doing something ineffective, we are being rude.

Because, when we tell someone to calm down, we are basically telling her that she doesn't have legitimate reasons for being worked up, which usually only makes her more frustrated.

This is our least effective (and most commonly used) technique.

WAITING

This is when we think that time equates to calmness. The problem is that time doesn't make us calmer. In fact, it often only makes us more upset, because we don't spend that time allowing the calming process to occur. We spend it dwelling on our fears and frustrations. If we're not careful, time will only fan the flame of our bad emotions -- giving them power to keep us worked up.

SOLITUDE

This is when we think that being alone will make us calmer. It doesn't really ensure that we've stopped raging. It only ensures that we aren't sharing our space with anyone while we do it. If we want solitude to help us, we can't just distance ourselves from other people; we must also distance ourselves from those destructive thoughts and feelings that keep us excited.

PRETENDING

This is when we try to act like nothing's bothering us. It usually provides an instant sense of relief, albeit a frail one. Because, it really just makes us more fragile. More afraid of our bubble being popped, which is threatened by all the real things we find bothersome.

ELIMINATING PROVOCATION

This is when we try to shelter ourselves from what is bothering us. The issue with this is that we allow ourselves not to deal with the real problem. And, we often end up eliminating challenges that could strengthen us, as well as people who we would be better off having by our sides.

ESCAPING

This is when we try to numb our discomfort with false anesthetics. We turn to junk food, video games, internet-surfing, or even drugs and alcohol. It doesn't offer real improvement, because real solutions don't just help us escape our problems; they help us deal with them.

AGGRESSION

This is when we attempt to relieve our stress by becoming hostile -- usually, towards whatever we view is the source of our stress. While there are some healthy ways to take out aggression, such as beating on a drum set or a boxing bag, it is very easy to misplace our aggression unhealthily, adding more damage to what has already been done.

RECIPROCATING BAD BEHAVIOR

This is when we attempt to fight chaos with chaos. Your kid throws a tantrum, and you throw a tantrum back. Your husband gets loud and crazy, and you get even louder and crazier. In the movies, it works. In real life, emotional problems don't go away by bringing more emotional problems into the equation. The only real cure for chaos is order. We can only improve a bad situation by bringing to it what it is lacking.

MAKING UP FOR IT LATER

This is when we think we can reset the balance in our lives by making up for our bad moments with good moments. After we flip out at our spouse or scream at our kids, we decide to go above and beyond. Maybe we make a nice dinner. Maybe we take our kids to the fair and buy them toys and ice cream. The problem with this is that it fixes what isn't broken and fails to fix what ***is***. Because, the problem in our lives isn't that our good moments aren't good enough; it's that our bad moments are really bad. So bad, that they spill toxicity into all of the other moments in our lives. They create 99% of the regret and remorse that we walk around with the rest of the time. The other major problem with this thinking is that it is self-enabling. It allows us to continue our bad behavior -- falsely assured that there is no need for us to practice restraint in the present moment.

THE STUFF THAT WORKS

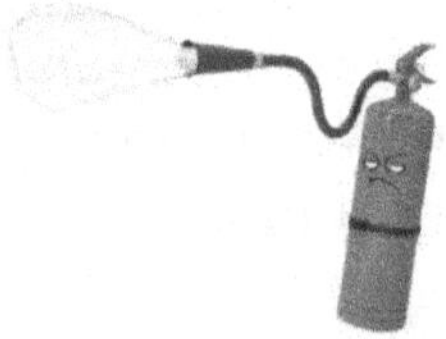

So then, how exactly DO we become calmer? I believe that secret lies, not in any one remedy, but in a combination of them. This is because the problem is multifaceted. It is not just psychological. Not just chemical. Not just physical. It is often all of these things.

In a story I recently heard, a woman took shelter under a bridge after hearing the sound of a tornado siren. There, she huddled in a safe corner, trembling with fear. Thinking about the worst. She truly thought she was at her life's end.

After some time, she realized that there was no wind. Cars were passing by. Clouds were breaking up, and a kid was out playing with his dog. A nice man told her that the siren had only been a routine test. And yet, that didn't seem to help her emotions. Inside, she was still unable to calm down for some time; even though she now knew for sure that the threat was never real.

This showed me that calming down is more than merely a matter of convincing our minds that all is well. It involves changes that take place in us chemically and physically. As long as there is a storm that's raging on inside us, it doesn't matter what the facts are. The problem within us remains unsolved.

The following is a list of useful exercises and remedies for calming down. Some focus on calming your mind. Others affect your body. Some target both. Some are supplements, which can be taken in many ways -- diffused, ingested, or absorbed through the skin. Altogether, they can be broken down into three main types: ***physical, mental, and supplemental.***

For best results, I recommend combining these different types of remedies. Do something that calms your mind, but also, do something that calms the tension in your muscles and helps your body reduce cortisol. Just as the problem is multifaceted, so should your solution(s) be as well.

You'll see that I have placed all the different supplements together into one exercise. I did this because I do not know which supplements (if any) will work for you. I'm not a doctor. I just know that, if you do choose to take supplements, they alone should not be perceived as a cure-all. Each one only aims at solving a single aspect of the problem, rather than addressing it fully.

If you happened to skip right to this section of the book, then I take it that you are pretty worked up right now. Your world may be turning red. You may be feeling as though you are losing control. Does that sound about right? If so, press pause.

Take a moment to assess your situation. What is the problem? What's at stake? Have you done or said anything yet that could be damaging? Hopefully, you have not. But, if you have, don't worry. It's not too late to start turning things around. Now is always the right time to start practicing prevention -- even if it feels like it's too late!

While it may seem like you have a lot to worry about right now, try to focus on your emotions. They represent a very crucial problem -- one that may need your attention more than any other problem. Solving this problem will help keep your situation from getting worse. And, put you in a better state of mind to solve whichever other problems you are facing.

Please take your time with each exercise. Don't just give them a half-hearted try and then say they didn't work. Also, I would recommend moving on if an exercise doesn't seem to be helping. The goal here is to figure out what works for you. And, what doesn't.

If you have the right mindset and motivation, I trust that you will find at least one exercise here that is helpful. For best results, skim over them all really quickly. Then, come back to the ones that stood out to you as helpful.

Once you've narrowed in on a single one or two, attack with your undivided focus, attention, and energy. You may even want to re-read an exercise multiple times if you aren't getting the desired effect.

Remember that it's common for us to quit trying when we don't see instant results. But, it's not that the solutions are ineffective; it's that ***we*** aren't applying them effectively, persistently, or wholeheartedly. Most solutions really only fail us when we give up on them.

THE IMPORTANCE OF STARTING WITH DESIRE

As we've already discussed, there is a big difference between knowing you need to calm down and actually wanting to. And, this may be the single most important distinction in this entire book.

Many of us know we need to calm down and go through all the motions of calming down. We are motivated by strong senses of guilt, fear or obligation. But this rarely is enough to truly help us. The part of us that wants to stay angry almost always overpowers the part of us that wants to calm down.

To make things harder, we are great at tricking ourselves into thinking that we want to calm down when we actually have no interest in it. If you are serious about making changes, then you probably need to do some honest, reflective soul-searching. Because if, in your heart of hearts, you still want to stay upset, that is your primary problem. It's the one that needs to be addressed before any other. I cannot overemphasize the importance this.

You need to create a shift in your desires so that you actually ***want*** to become calmer. To do this, I recommend that you reread the original lists I asked you to make at the beginning of this book. Explore your original reasons for wanting to buy this book. And, explore some of the regret you've felt in the past after acting on bad impulses. This will be the good fuel you need to fill your motivational tank.

Also, reread the section on misconceptions. Figure out which myth it is that you're believing and spot the bad logic in it. Hopefully that will make objective truth look a little more alluring. And, put you in the mood to let go of that rusty pole!

The following exercises are divided up into five groups.

They are:

- **STARTER EXERCISES**
- **PSYCHOLOGICAL EXERCISES**
- **PHYSICAL EXERCISES**
- **INTENSE PHYSICAL EXERCISES**
- **HERBAL SUPPLEMENTS**

STARTER EXERCISES

This first group of exercises is aimed at helping you create that shift in your desire. If any part of you is still on the fence (or not quite sure), this is probably a great place to start.

1. THE MIRROR

The "Gist" of it: In this exercise, you are simply taking the focus off of whatever you are upset about and placing it on yourself.

Why it's important: It's important because it puts you in the right frame of mind for any and all other exercises. It also brings your attention back to the thing that needs fixing. And, the thing you can control -- you!

In his book, *Why Marriages Succeed or Fail*, author John Gottman talks about certain couples who have agreed to be observed during intense marital arguments. These couples have cameras watching their movements and medical equipment attached to them to monitor their physiological changes.

They begin talking about normal things -- the weather, the news, etc. Eventually, they come to a subject that one or both of them feels passionately about. As they slowly start to get worked up, their body language changes. They start to fidget and take aggressive, defensive postures. Their heart rates go up and their vocal speeds and pitches change. And yet, most of them aren't at all aware of these changes as they are happening. They have to watch the videos of themselves just to see the signs and symptoms on display, which are things that seem obvious to anybody else watching.

The goal of the exercise is to help train people to focus on themselves. Because, they are often too focused on the person or thing that upset them. Too fixated on another person's actions to see that their own actions need restabilizing. You know that your spouse needs to calm down. But, shouldn't you calm down too? Shouldn't you calm down first?

Has it ever made the situation better to focus on his mood? Has it ever worked out for you when you've shouted, "You're acting crazy! Calm down?" Hasn't that always just made the both of you more excited? The solution is not to focus on him, or on any other bother or frustration around you. Rather, the solution is to focus on ***you***.

There are many reasons why this can help. One, is that we tend to want to fix what we are focusing on. When you sit in front of an unfinished jigsaw puzzle, you instantly start trying to find where the missing pieces go. Stare at a crooked picture frame, and you instinctively want to reach over and straighten it. It is almost as though we don't know how not to make improvements to the thing we are focusing on.

Focus on yourself, and the same is true -- you instantly start to see where you yourself need straightening. You begin to notice all of your own missing pieces, and you cultivate a need and desire to fill them in. This effect can be both powerful and positive.

However, it can be very negative when we focus on the wrong thing. When you look at things that you have no power to change, such as your wife, you typically only become more worked up and irritated. You make her faults seem larger than they are. You make yourself want to straighten her out and find all of her missing pieces, which is both futile and destructive.

Right now, you may not recognize the subtle ways that your upsetness is affecting you. You may be like those spouses who are being monitored, who focus on every problem except the one in themselves. You may feel sure that someone or something else is what needs fixing. But what needs fixing is you. Turn your attention on yourself. Work on you.

As difficult as this is, there is a certain beauty to it. It offers personal growth that doesn't depend on anyone or anything else. Even if your wife never stops trying to give you directions while you're driving, and even if your teenage son never stops acting like a know-it-all, you can change your response. That is as important as anything that can happen to you.

HOW TO DO IT

Pause for a moment. Try to find a nice, calm place in your vicinity where you have some space and time to reflect. Then, try to notice which thoughts and feelings are going through you right now. How might you describe them? As angry? Rageful? Irritated? How would you describe your state of mind? Startled? Cornered? Stunned? And, how would you describe your disposition overall?

How does it feel to focus on yourself? Perhaps, it invokes guilt. Maybe you were taught not to think too much or too highly of yourself, and a self-focus feels, well... selfish. Maybe you've grown up believing that anger and fear are bad emotions, and it's easier to deny those feelings than face them. Or, maybe you feel that it's silly to focus on how you feel -- like doing so makes you a wimp or a pansy.

If so, try to realize what the real threat is here -- it has nothing to do with looking silly or wimpy. It has to do with failing to recognize your tough emotions and failing to work through them.

As you spot your negative emotions, try to see how they are separate from you. They are not a defining part of you. They are just there -- like signs, making suggestions. And, you do not have to do as they are suggesting. You can simply observe them. You can even be entertained by them.

Note: This probably won't be easy, because you'll be tempted to shift your focus away from your emotions and onto the person or thing that you think caused them. That would not be productive. The goal, remember, is to keep your eyes on you; not on some other person or thing.

You may even find it helpful to look in the mirror while you do this exercise. What do you see? Answer the following questions:

1. What is my facial expression?
2. What signs or symptoms of anxiety are currently showing?
3. Which emotions might be behind those signs and symptoms?
4. What is my body language?
5. What is my posture? Am I tense and rigid, or relaxed and at ease?
6. What sensations are going on inside me? Am I balanced, or am I off kilter?

Next, try to correct anything that is off.

Do you see a furrowed brow? Try to relax it.

Are your hands shaking? Try to steady them.

Are you breathing quickly? Try to control your breaths.

Is your heart racing? Try to sit down and relax your body. Return balance to anything that is imbalanced.

Congratulations. You have found the root of the problem. Great news... it's one that you can fix!

2. THE INCENTIVIZER

The "Gist" of it: With this exercise, you are simply coming up with ***NEW*** incentives to stay calm.

Why it's important: It's important because we tend to lose most of our good incentives when we get worked up. And, without them, we become extremely susceptible to making bad choices.

If you're upset now, there's a good chance that you want to stay angry. There's a good chance that you aren't really interested in calming down or in doing what's wise or in doing what truly will make for a better future. In fact, all those ideas may sound like lofty, fluffy nonsense.

So then, how can you become more positively motivated? How can you find good incentives when there don't seem to be any in sight? The answer is simple -- you can make your own. That's right, you can become more positively motivated right now.
You can create a brand-new goal for yourself that offers you a reward you want -- one that lures you in a more positive direction and steers you away from chaos. And, by doing this, you will reward yourself doubly.

You will not only avoid the headache that your current path was leading you to, you will rediscover the peace, the clarity, and the joy that can come from doing what's right, rather than doing what feels good. Plus, keep in mind that you will be stepping closer to that reward that you have created for yourself, whatever that may be. A good new incentive will actually give you reason to start doing what's in your best interest right now.

HOW TO DO IT

For starters, think of something fun -- something that you'd really like to do, but haven't allowed yourself. Perhaps, because you haven't been able to justify spending the time or the money. Maybe you've always wanted to go to a comedy club. Maybe you've wanted to treat yourself to a professional massage. Well, guess what... you're in luck! Now is the time to allow yourself that thing you've been saying no to. But, under one condition -- you have to calm down right now!

Now, create a set of rules that must be kept in order for you to claim the prize. For example, you might say, "In order to claim this prize, I must..."

a. Refrain from being sarcastic.
b. Resist the urge to act aggressively.
c. Keep from raising my voice.

d. Keep from saying or doing anything out of anger.
e. Keep from thinking about the thing that's bothering me.

You may even decide upon a time frame that establishes how long these rules must be followed. You might say "I need to successfully calm down within ______ minutes, without returning to a worked-up state for a total of _________ hours." Being as specific as possible will help define what you can and cannot do. And, increase the odds that your incentives will be strong enough to guide you in the right direction.

3. THE GOAL SCALE

The "Gist" of it: In this exercise, you are attempting to calm down by evaluating how your current situation is connected to your true-life goals.

Why it's important: It's important because anger has a way of making us forget what we really want.

Right now, you may be angry at your spouse for some of the things she's done or said. Maybe, you're tempted to hurt her back. Maybe, you genuinely want to make her feel the same type of pain that she has inflicted on you. And, while these desires may feel genuine, they probably don't represent what you truly want most for yourself or for her.

Think about why you married her. You must have had a reason, and it probably wasn't so that you'd have someone to take your anger out on. It wasn't so that you'd have someone to win fights with, or someone to look better than. You married her for other reasons. You loved her. You wanted to experience the joys of a mutually satisfying (but hard-earned) type of bond. You had better goals. You just can't see them right now. Revisiting your real goals can make you smarter about handling your situation.

This exercise probably won't teach you anything new; it will simply help you discover what you already know -- that deeper, richer knowledge that's in you, which has become dormant. As Galileo once said, "You cannot teach a man anything; you can only help him find it within himself."

Think about the things you care most about in life. What really matters to you? Is it family, faith, and friends? Is it living a good life, or leaving a lasting legacy? Get back in touch with what really matters to you and choose actions that are congruent with your values. Choose to see how doing what feels good might be jeopardizing to your truer, more meaningful goals. Never are you in greater need of reexamining your goals than when you are worked up -- tempted to act in ways that would sabotage them.

Right now, if you pause to really think about it, you'll find that there's something you care about more than getting revenge. Something you want more than winning a fight. Something you want more than serving justice. And, it's something that will come at the cost of getting what feels good now. As the saying goes, "Sometimes you have to pass up what you want now... to get what you want even more."

HOW TO DO IT

This exercise works best if you have something you can look at that stirs up positive feelings. An old letter. A piece of jewelry. A poem, a keepsake, or a journal entry that you wrote long ago when you were in a better state of mind. If possible, find such a thing and reflect on it for a while.

Be alone with your old self. Be alone with that part of you that wants something better than the despairing, vengeful, or destructive goals you've been distracted by. What do you ***REALLY*** want? How can this moment play a role in bringing you closer to what you truly find meaningful? Reflect until you actually ***REMEMBER*** what you find meaningful. Don't let the frustration of the present moment trick you, the way it does so many people.

As you put forth energy in this, you will find a few things happening: one, the time you spend thinking will activate your brain, and you won't just be relying on your animal instincts. You'll automatically start wanting to make smarter choices. Second, you'll start to come back in touch with better emotions. You will form a desire to be calm. And, you'll be one large step closer to being there. Give it a try!

Here are a few questions you may want to ask yourself:

1. When was the last time I truly felt clear about what I wanted in life?
2. What was it that I saw during that moment?
3. How did that desire conflict with my current desires?
4. Which of those conflicting desires can I eliminate in order to realign myself with my more positive goals?

4. THE SPELL-CHECKER

The "Gist" of it: In this exercise, you are spelling out your thoughts and feelings and checking them to see if they stand up to logic.

Why it's important: It's important because we so often fail to truly know our thoughts and feelings, or to see the fallacies in them.

Right now, you're worked up. That may be the only thing that feels certain. You hit your thumb with a hammer, and now, you want to throw that hammer at the wall with all of your might. But, do you really understand why? Probably not. Part of the reason you're so worked up is because you are able to feel your feelings much better than you are able to understand them.

As it turns out, you're not really upset at the hammer. Nor are you upset at the wall that you're tempted to throw it at. The things you're tempted to lash out at aren't even remotely related to your frustrations. And, if you dug a little deeper, you'd see this. You might even find out why you're really angry. That understanding would help you feel less confusion. And, as a result, less frustration.

While it may not be easy right now, it would benefit you to pause and test your thoughts and feelings.

You may realize that they sound like total gibberish once you try to articulate them. What happens to your logic when it is exposed to the harsh, telling light of reality? You won't know until you bring it out of hiding.

HOW TO DO IT

In your head (or aloud), spell out your feelings. You can do so by finishing the following sentences:

1. At the root of my upsetness, I feel ________.
2. I feel this way because ____________.
3. These feelings are tempting me to ____________.
4. I think that if I do________, it will cause ________ to happen.
5. I think that my bad actions would be justifiable because ____________.
6. A better course of action might be to ____________ instead.

Note: You may even want to write these answers out on paper, which will increase the chances of spotting fallacies in them. Seeing your thoughts on paper may shine some extra light on them. Hopefully, you will begin to feel calmer as you start to see beyond your feelings and understand how they are influencing you.

This may be difficult because we tend to latch onto false narratives when we are upset or hurting -- ones that offer us justification and validation. The part of us that enjoys delusional thinking is the same part that fights us tooth and nail whenever we try to see our emotions objectively.

It may help you to remember that most of our bad choices in life come this way -- by consciously allowing ourselves to quit thinking. It's why so many intelligent people do stupid things that go against their logic and intelligence. The same could easily be true for you. Are the actions you're considering contradictory to your sound logic?

Your main enemy here is not a lack of understanding, but rather, a refusal to acknowledge your understanding. Not an inability to think, but rather, a temporary refusal to think.

As Ben Franklin once said, "We are all born ignorant, but one must work hard to remain stupid." When you're worked up, you're working pretty hard to maintain a limited focus. The answer: stop working so hard!

Let go of those silly ideas that are floating in your head right now.

While they're tempting to latch onto, it is in your best interest to return to the good logic that goes against the destructive, negative emotions you are tempted to act upon.

5. THE NEW ANGLE

The "Gist" of it: In this exercise, you are changing your vantage point to see your problem from a new angle.

Why it's important: It's important because your current upsetness is probably harming your outlook on life.

Being worked up makes you more prone to making hasty generalizations. More prone to seeing things through a negative lens. You notice the half of the glass that's less full. The portion of grass that's less green. And, you overlook a lot of the positive.

A large part of the problem is the way you see the problem. And, while this may not seem like good news, it actually is; it implies that you can actually improve your situation simply by choosing to see it differently.

Of course, this isn't easy, because you'd rather not be seeing your problem at all! It is unwelcome. Unwanted. It seems unworthy of your precious time and energy. And yet, if you fail to give it your time and energy, it will only end up lingering longer -- doing more damage than it should. It would be better to stop resisting your problem and give it the mental energy that it requires. You can start by seeing it from a new angle.

HOW TO DO IT

Try to think of different ways to perceive your frustrating situation. Ones that you may not have noticed at first. You may want to ask yourself these questions:

- *Are there any positive aspects to my problem that I may not be seeing? Any ways it could be benefiting me or someone else? Could it hold a valuable lesson?*
- *Is there anyone I know who has been in a situation like this before? Did they handle it better than me? Did they handle it worse? What might I be able to learn from their experience?*
- *How can my situation teach me to be grateful? How can it educate me? How might it be making me more flexible and adaptable? Could it be making me more empathetic, more patient, or more understanding? Could this speedbump be used as a ramp to launch me higher and further?*
- *What is my situation telling me about my anger? Does it show me that I have nobody but myself to be upset with, and that my anger is misdirected?*

- *Could my misfortune have prevented some other misfortune -- one that would have been even greater and even more catastrophic?*
- *Could there be a humorous side to it all? Could it contain the essence of a great story that not only makes people laugh, but also, helps them understand how to avoid or deal with similar frustrations in their own lives?*

Try to think of at least three new angles to see your problem from -- ones that will give you a better, more objective view. Doing this is like getting paid after a hard day's work. You've already done the hard part – you've endured the frustration. Now, do the rewarding part! Find the gold in the pan of dirt you've been holding!

6. THE TIME-LAPSE

The "Gist" of it: In this exercise, you are seeing how your current frustration compares to a past frustration -- one that you once thought was big but now think is small.

Why it's important: It's important because reflecting on past experiences can give us perspective in the present.

There is something about the present moment that puts a blur in our perspectives. It causes us to exaggerate our frustrations. To overestimate the magnitude of our problems. Never are we worse at evaluating a moment than when we are in it. Never are we more prone to making mountains out of molehills.

In third grade, you spilled lemonade on your pants. You were so embarrassed. You stood there at the end of the lunch line with a large wet spot on your crotch, as the rest of the class roared in laughter. You thought it was the end of the world. You didn't think you'd ever outlive it, and no one could have convinced you otherwise.

Now though, you can laugh about it. It doesn't even seem like a big deal. In fact, it's hard for you to see why it ever did. It all just begs the question -- could your current situation be similar? Could it be just another overinflated concern that time will naturally deflate? Something you look back on years later only to wonder why it ever once mattered?

The thing is, you probably won't be able to remember ***WHY*** you were upset. But you will most likely remember ***WHAT*** you damaged. ***WHO*** you hurt. ***WHERE*** you were when it happened, and ***WHEN*** your regret began. To keep your frustrations from turning into regret, try to realize that what you're feeling now will most likely fade. Let's talk more about how this is done.

HOW TO DO IT

This exercise can be done in your head, although it works better if you have a piece of paper and something to write with.

1. Draw a horizontal line all the way across your piece of paper (or, just imagine one, if you are doing this exercise in your head).
2. Now, try to think of one very frustrating event from your past -- one that once seemed big, but now seems small. Imagine that that is what this timeline represents.
3. Beneath the far-left end of that line, write the words, "The way I felt in the moment."
4. Underneath that, write down some adjectives that describe how you felt about that old frustration at the time. You may use such words as "huge, daunting, catastrophic, embarrassing, or painful."
5. Now, go to the far-right end of that line and write the words, "The way I felt long afterwards."
6. Underneath that, write down the appropriate adjectives that describe your feelings later on. You may use words such as "small, petty, irrelevant, funny, or comical." You may also

write down any things you did or said that you eventually came to regret.

7. Write down what you could have done better, and how you wish you would have handled it. Write down what the wiser, more mature actions would have been. Be specific.
8. Now, use this same timeline to represent your current frustration. Let it show you the diminishing power that time can have on your emotions -- including those emotions you are feeling at present. Let it remind you of the inevitable path your current bad emotions will take you on, should you act on them. Let it remind you that there is a better way to handle your situation -- one that you won't be as regretful about later on. These realizations should help you to figure out a better way forward, and to feel calmer about your current situation.

7. THE GRATEFUL TOUCH

The "Gist" of it: In this exercise, you are attempting to calm down by focusing on what you have to be grateful for.

Why it's important: It's important because gratitude invokes good feelings, and good feelings promote good desires and good actions.

Not long ago, I read about a tennis player whose nervousness used to overcome him before big matches. He was told by a fellow player that he should try to "Play with gratefulness." Feeling that there wasn't anything to lose, he decided to give it a try.

Before his next match, he began to feel those same familiar nervous feelings. So, he began to shift his attention towards things he was grateful for. He focused on his health and his family and any other blessing he could think of. Soon, his disposition changed.

He felt calmer inside. He could focus better. He was able to play with greater control. And, as the story goes, he won that match. And, the one after. He was soon beating people that had defeated him in years prior. What he learned is that focusing on your blessings is a great way to calm your nerves.

Being grateful does something good to us. It lifts our spirits and our outlooks above our circumstances and allows us to see outside our tainted perspective lenses. It causes a shift in our attitudes for the better. But, it does even more than that.

Because, to focus on the good, we must be in the present. Being grateful demands a certain amount of concentration from us -- a level that we cannot give if we aren't in the here and now. And, by being in the "Here and now," we become present with other virtues, such as love, kindness, compassion, and honesty. This may be why Cicero once said that "Gratitude is not only the greatest of virtues, but the parent of all others."

The present is the only real moment. It's the only place where choices can be made, and actions can be taken. It's the only place where happiness can be felt, and life can be experienced. Gratefulness brings us back to it when we've wandered.

HOW TO DO IT

Simply pause and try to think of at least three things you can be grateful for. Ideally, it would be even better to try to come up with 5 or more. Doing this has the potential to change your mindset and calm any nerves you may be feeling.

It is important to note that you don't have to be grateful for your misfortunes; just find a way to be grateful in spite of them. Just because bad things are happening, doesn't mean you need to adopt a bad perspective.

Be grateful for the damage that wasn't done. Be grateful that your frustrations didn't start sooner. Be grateful that they didn't last longer. You can be glad for such simple things as the weather or the scenery or a smile that a stranger gave you. If you look for things to be grateful for, you should be able to find at least a few. And, this should help you to calm down.

8. THE PIGGYBACK

The "Gist" of it: This exercise aims to help you tap into the power of other people as a source of motivation.

Why it's important: It's important because we are often willing to do more for others than we are for ourselves.

In world war II, Austrian Holocaust survivor, Viktor frankl, had a realization about his fellow POWs. He noticed that the ones who stayed mentally strong were the ones who had someone other than themselves to care for. They were responsible -- not just for their own well-being, but for the well-being of another person.

This amazing realization showed him that survival wasn't really about being the fittest or the strongest; it was about having a reason to stay strong. Or, to say it better, having somebody other than yourself to stay strong for.

It showed him that other people have the ability to help us tap into a reservoir of strength within us that we cannot easily access on our own. We can only access it with the help of others. With their help, we give more. We try harder. We last longer. Isn't it true that you give just a little more effort when you know that your kids, neighbors, or coworkers are watching?

This is the strange phenomenon that Jordan Peterson is pointing to in his book, Twelve rules for life. His second rule, "Treat yourself like someone you are responsible for helping," indicates that when it is for more than our own good, we always seem to perform just a little bit better.

How might this benefit you right now? How could it help you see the bigger picture and form a desire to do what's right? Hopefully, you are able to use somebody else to tap into that reservoir of strength within you.

HOW TO DO IT

Try to imagine someone you love feeling the way you feel right now. Imagine that they are in the exact same position, feeling the exact same way. It's YOUR job to inform them of the correct way of acting. What are some of the basic, wise pieces of advice that you would be able to say to them without even having to think about it?

Now, comes the hard part. Imagine that it's your turn to take that same advice. You are fully aware of what you should do. You've just proven that you know where the line is and how not to cross it. Can you take your own advice? If not for yourself, could you do it for someone you love?

Yes, you can. Even if that person isn't watching, you can imagine that he/she is. Truthfully though, somebody probably is watching -- whether you know it or not. And, your character matters -- whether or not you even have an audience.

9. THE DISTORTION FINDER

The "Gist" of it: in this exercise, you are looking for non-helpful connections that are affecting the way you think.

Why it's important: This is important because our minds tend to distort the data we take in.

Here are fifteen of the most common cognitive distortions that we experience. As you read through the list, please try to see if you find yourself falling victim to any of these distortions. And, if so, try to see how they may be contributing to any of your bad emotions.

If you discover that you are prone to any of these cognitive distortions, try to recognize how they are affecting your perspectives. And, try to recognize how the real truth is different from your distorted view of it.

Catastrophizing

This is when a person assumes the worst-case-scenario based on a single negative factor. For example, a woman may see water on her floor and assume she has a leaky roof, and that she will probably have to sell her house because she can't afford to get it fixed.

Realistically, that may not be true. The water may be from a glass of water that spilled and dripped from the table. It might not have anything to do with the bad scenario that she is imagining.

All-or-Nothing Thinking

This distortion, also known as "Black-and-White Thinking," makes it hard to see a full spectrum of possibilities. You either see things as being all one way or all another, as though there are no in betweens. You may think, "Either I will do well on this test, or I will completely fail as a student." But chances are good that there are quite a few possibilities outside that.

Disqualifying the Positive

In this distortion, you give credit only to the negative things that happen in your life. If a positive thing does occur, you reject it as coincidental, accidental, or unrepresentative of the norm. This distortion could be behind any negative perspectives you may be carrying about life, causing you to think that it is unobjective or unrealistic to acknowledge things that are positive.

Control Fallacies

Control fallacies tend to manifest themselves in one of two ways. Either we believe that we have no control whatsoever in our situations, or we believe we have complete control over everything that happens to us. Neither belief is accurate. For example, even though we may feel like we are completely in control of ourselves, we cannot control our surroundings or how others' actions may affect us. Or, if we think we have no control of our situation whatsoever, we still have control in how we choose to perceive it and how to react to it.

Overgeneralization

This distortion focuses on a single example and uses it to assume an overall pattern. For example, Chairman Mao, the infamous communist dictator of China, once came to the mathematical conclusion that 10% of the population were rightists who had to be dealt with punitively. Based upon this, he divided the population into groups of one hundred, assuming that ten rightists could be found in every one-hundred-person group. Of course, this was flawed in many ways. Mathematically, it was flawed in the way that the ten percent figure was merely an average -- not accounting for the uniqueness of each one-hundred-person group. In some groups, there were no rightists. In others, there were far more than 10. But, because of this overgeneralization, many people were unfairly condemned as rightists. In the same way, you and I can easily overgeneralize random samples of data in our lives and from inaccurate conclusions about reality.

Minimization

Minimization is sometimes known as the "Binocular Trick," because it is like looking backward through binoculars. You see all the important details as teeny, tiny specs. An example of this would be a runner who wins an elite award, but downplays the importance of the award, continuing to think he is average.

Mind Reading

This distortion manifests in the assumption that a person knows what others are thinking. Of course, no one can. Sometimes we ***think*** we know what another person is thinking, but none of us truly know another's thoughts or motives, and we can easily end up at some bad conclusions about people by doing this.

Fallacy of Change

Blamers commonly use this distortion. It consists of believing that your own personal happiness depends on the people around you to change. You believe that in order for you to feel happy, your wife has to do X or Y, or your children have to adopt different (or less irritating) habits.

Fortune Telling

This distortion involves making predictions that are based on little (or no) evidence. For example, going by the fact that you spilled coffee on your shirt this morning and arrived late to work, you believe you can safely assume that nothing will go your way for the rest of the day. You feel 100% certain of this, based on nothing more than the fact that a few negative events have already transpired.

Emotional Reasoning

This is when we mistake our feelings for reality. The logic we use with this distortion is that our emotions are the same as facts. If we are afraid, we see our fear as evidence of real danger. If we suspect somebody of having ill-intent toward us, we see our suspicions as evidence of that person's bad intentions. I don't trust her. Therefore, she must not be trustworthy. We believe that if we feel strongly enough about something, it therefore must be true.

Always Being Right

This distortion exists in one's belief that he must always be right. Where other reasonable people would accept a difference of opinion and "agree to disagree," a person with this distortion will carry on long past the point of productive discussion, battling to the metaphorical death.

Personalization

This distortion has to do with taking things personally -- even when there is no personal attachment. For example, you may assume that it rained in a city because you were there, or that the smoke from a campfire favors you more than the others sitting around the fire.

You may assume that the people around you would be enjoying their time more if you weren't there, or that their instances of moodiness or irritation are somehow because of you.

Should Statements

Should statements are statements that we typically make about others or ourselves regarding ideals that we think should be met. Some of the expectations we make are judgmental, unreasonable, and unsubstantial. For example, a man might say, "Normal people should be married and finished with school by the time they are thirty." Of course, it's easy to see how such a statement could cause guilt, disappointment, and anger when this expectation is not lived up to.

Fallacy of Fairness

While fairness is something we all would like, we live in a world that is anything but fair. And, if we expect life to be fair, we are more likely to harbor negative feelings when we inevitably encounter the many unfairnesses of life.

Heaven's Reward Fallacy

This distortion manifests itself in the belief that a person's struggles, trials, and efforts will ultimately result in a great reward of some kind. The problem is that hard work and sacrifice do not always pay off, and this is easy to prove. And, in those situations when hard work and good intentions don't pay off, a person may experience even greater disappointment, frustration, or anger than he/she would have without such lofty expectations.

HOW TO DO IT

Using the above list of distortions, identify your own unique patterns of thinking, behaving, and feeling. Also, try to recognize the significance that any of your distortions have on your perspective of reality. Finally, do your best to form a more well-rounded perspective of reality, taking into account your own unique tendencies. This will help you replace inaccurate perspectives with ones that are more accurate.

PSYCHOLOGICAL EXERCISES

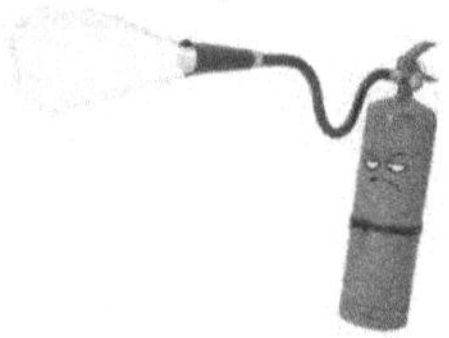

These exercises are primarily psychological. They deal with the part of the problem that is simpler to solve -- the part that exists in your head. One main benefit of these exercises is that they can be practiced anywhere. Anytime. They are also fairly fast-acting -- working as quickly as your ability to focus. One weakness, however, is that they depend on your ability to focus, which is often greatly compromised by high states of emotion.

We should also note that these exercises probably will not have much of an effect on the physical component of your excitedness, and that, even if you apply them successfully, you will still need to find a physical exercise of your choosing to pair them with. I recommend pairing them with the Notebook, the Yoga Mat, or the Sweat Breaker. Any of these will address the physical component of your excitedness, making you more well-balanced overall.

10. THE ZOOM-OUT

The "Gist" of it: In this exercise, you are trying to see how your focus may be distorting reality. And, you are seeking to zoom out and expand your overall view.

Why it's important: It's important because we are greatly influenced by what we focus on. Focus determines how we see, what we see, and what we ***DON'T*** see.

Have you ever noticed how a single event can set the tone for your entire day? You find a five-dollar bill, and suddenly you find yourself humming a happy tune. You're smiling more and acting kinder to strangers. Or, you get a flat tire, and you suddenly find yourself noticing ten other things that are wrong in the world. What can explain this phenomenon? Focus. Focus tends to influence how we see everything else.

However, the influence given to us by our focus usually isn't objective. It tends to be based on a view of only part of reality's spectrum, rather than all of it. It's kind of like looking at something through a microscope. You get a great view of a tiny aspect of it, but you get a very poor view that object as a whole.

The same is true about the view you have of your life when something is frustrating you. When your husband is disrespectful to you. When the department store won't honor your receipt. When your dog poops on the living room carpet. You have a crystal-clear view of the thing that's bothering you. But, your unfettering gaze upon that thing makes it seem bigger than it is, and you need objectivity. You need to zoom out. Once you do, you will expand your focus, and your frustration will automatically shrink to it appropriate size.

Caution: this is not easy. In fact, some part of you probably takes some comfort in zooming in on the negative. Self-pity offers a sense of justification. It lets you keep on believing that you are a victim and someone else is the villain. Just try to realize that such distorted focuses do not actually benefit you. You'll benefit more by being objective. You'll benefit more by zooming out.

HOW TO DO IT

Ask yourself:

- What is at the center point of my focus right now?
- Does this thing deserve to be the center point of my focus?
- How might it be negatively influencing the way I think and feel overall?
- Which other things in my view has it kept me from noticing?
- What might I have hoped to gain by zooming in on this one thing?
- How might my narrow perspective be hurting me overall?

NOTE: you may have to temporarily step away from your surroundings if they make it hard to zoom out. While this is a mental exercise, it may require you to zoom out physically as well.

11. THE CONCEPT CRUSHER

The "Gist" of it: In this exercise, you are trying to differentiate between real threats and perceived threats.

Why it's important: This is important because there is usually a big difference between threats that are real and threats that we think are real.

A lot of times, our thoughts and concepts about reality are much different than reality itself. Our minds put their own spin on it. We incorporate our own superstitions and develop interpretations that are influenced by our moods. We can easily end up with irrational, unwarranted fears that keep us from being in the here and now. If you are feeling worked up now, there is a good chance that your view of reality may be in danger -- skewed by your intense emotions and your inability to see how they are affecting you.

You may think that the sky is falling, when realistically, you may have only felt a drop of rain. You may think that you are going to lose your job, when realistically, your boss simply didn't say hi to you when you passed him in the hallway. Your mind can easily jump to conclusions about threats that may not even be real.

Of course, some of your threats may be real, but that is even more reason why you should get out of your head and be mentally present -- seeing reality for what it is; rather than your own skewed version of it. Now, more than ever, you need to step out of your mind and re-enter the real world -- the one that isn't loosely held together by unregulated interpretations, invisible superstitions, and emotionally-driven exaggerations.

HOW TO DO IT

Look around you. Try to find something in your surroundings that looks peaceful, such as a tree or a stone. Now, realize that that tree and that stone are real. They are separate from any thoughts or feelings you may have about them. They are here -- not in some other imaginary place. They are now -- not in some other past or future moment.

They are fixtures of the real reality -- not the one that your mind imagines. They are unaffected by the whirlwind of emotions within you. They lie there in the breeze, never worrying. Never bothered by the rise and fall of the stock market. They don't change or move when you get upset.

They sit there motionlessly, almost as though they are able to enjoy a much more peaceful, tranquil version of their surroundings -- one that you become detached from when you are trapped inside of your own mind.

Now, ask yourself: which version of reality am I currently in? The real one, or the one that is being distorted by my mind's conceptual lens? If it is the latter, try to spend a few moments rediscovering the real world -- the one that, up till now, has gone missing. Take comfort in any ways that the real reality is better, more peaceful, or more beautiful than the one in your head.

If you still can't determine whether a threat is real or imagined, you may try looking around you to see if anyone else shares your sense of urgency or cruciality. If you are the only one who is losing your peace of mind over the threats you perceive, it adds to the case that those threats may exist only in your head.

Know thyself. Know how your own emotions move you. Try to spot the patterns that so easily pull you away from the real reality and into the fabricated one. Learn how to get out of your mind once that has happened. Doing this will make you a better you. It will make you a calmer you.

12. THE REDIRECT

The "Gist" of it: This technique is similar to zooming out. Only, rather than zooming out, you are zooming in... on something else -- something good that invokes positive feelings!

Why it's important: It is important because it gives you yet another way of escaping the negativity of a bad focus.

Life seems to demand a certain amount of mental discipline from us. Without it, our thoughts can harm us. Some thoughts can make us more afraid. Some thoughts can make us more upset. Some thoughts can even make us feel physically sick. Obviously, bad thoughts have power. But the good news is that good thoughts have power too. Power to inspire. Power to give courage. Power to make us calm.

In order to tap into this good power, we usually have to find something outside of our immediate environments to focus on. A soldier at battle has to look beyond the ever-present sound of gunfire. A scared child has to look beyond the darkness in his room. Beyond the sights and sounds in front of us, we can usually find something better to focus on. Something that almost has a transforming effect on us.

As the old proverb says, "As a man thinketh, so is he." We are shaped by what we think of. So then... what are you thinking of? How is it shaping you? Or, to put it another way, how would you prefer to be shaped right now?

Would you like to be shaped into a calmer person? Think thoughts that inspire calmness. Would you like to be shaped into a braver person? Think thoughts that inspire bravery. It only requires that you be intentional. And, that you find thoughts to think that are better than the ones that come easy at present.

HOW TO DO IT

Find a thought that is more peaceful and happy. More calm and safe. One that brings you back in touch with some part of yourself that you currently feel out of touch with but would like to feel connected with again. Search through your memory banks. Think of moments you've lived through or books you've read that inspire the desired emotions. Let the thoughts about those things become stronger and more dominant than the negative thoughts.

Maybe your memory of graduating college reminds you of a time when you felt proud and strong. Maybe that trophy on your wall reminds you that you are capable of accomplishing great things when you put your mind to it. Such thoughts can offer calmness to you in your current situation. Such thoughts are more worthy of your attention and energy.

Devote some energy to finding good thoughts. And, devote some energy to focusing on them. It may take some persistence because you are interrupting your mind's patterns, which, like a river, are used to flowing a certain way. With a little work, you'll be able to get them to flow in a better direction.

13. THE OOH SHINY

The "Gist" of it: In this exercise, you are using a weakness (distraction) to your advantage.

Why it's important: It's important because, right now, any thought is probably better than the negative one that you're stuck on.

Fortunately, this is an easy method of escaping. So easy, that we tend to do it most when we aren't even trying. When we know we're supposed to be studying for a test or listening to a boring speaker. Our minds so easily wander off track.

Well, good news -- this is one instance where you don't WANT to stay on track. Right now, your mind is fixated on a single negative thought that is most likely perpetuating your upsetness. Distraction has the power to rescue you and break you out of that cycle.

Since your mind is incapable of thinking more than one thought at a time, choosing a good thought eliminates the possibility that a bad thought will dominate. By keeping a positive thought at the helm, you put yourself in a position where it is impossible to stay worked up.

HOW TO DO IT

As the exercise name "Ooh Shiny" suggests, look for something that catches your eye. It could be anything. The smooth surface of a railing or a flickering light. Let that object distract you and pull your mind it's way.

Get on Pinterest and browse the personal recommendations for you. Turn on the Xbox and allow yourself to waste some time. Right now, wasting time is probably a better alternative than keeping your negative focus. Try thinking of things that normally distract you. Do you know what they are?

Where does your mind typically go when it wanders off? On an adventure? To an old memory? Do you dream of riding on a train through the European countryside? Ok, great. Why not allow your mind to go there now? Drift off to that greener grass that you normally are tempted to wander to.

Engage yourself in some activity that requires your focus, such as a game of chess or a crossword puzzle. Do a tricky math problem or try asking yourself open-ended questions -- ones that require more than a simple yes or no answer. This should not only distract you, it should also free up the part of your mind that is good at problem-solving and finding solutions.

14. THE DELAY

The "Gist" of it: In this exercise, you are simply delaying your thoughts, words, and actions for a given amount of time.

Why it's important: It is important for four reasons. One, it prevents you from making emotionally driven choices. Two, it relieves you of the feeling of pressure to give an immediate response. Three, it gives you the assurance that your problem will be handled later on, by a calmer, more sensible you. Four, it lets you think about better things in the meantime.

Have you ever written an essay? If so, you most likely started with a rough draft. Then, you edited that rough draft over and over until it finally said what you wanted it to say. That editing took time, but it paid off. Well, that is the same concept that applies in this exercise. When we take time to edit our thoughts and actions, we usually come to much better decisions -- ones that better reflect us and better demonstrate our true feelings and desires.

Hindsight is 20/20. It shows us what we couldn't see in the moment. Most often, it shows us that we would have been better off taking no action at all, rather than acting according to how we felt during highly emotional situations. And, it shows us that our failure to do this is often our single greatest cause of regret.

Sometimes, success is as simple as waiting to respond. In games like chess, players often win -- not because they are smarter or more skilled than their opponents, but because they resist the urge to make hasty, poorly-thought out decisions. They outplay smarter players simply because they utilize the full amount of time they are given. In the end, we should remember that it doesn't matter how much time is left on the clock. What matters is how well we played with the time we had. Are there any areas of life that waiting will make you a better player in?

This one small thing can improve your chances of making better life choices. It can free up your mind to think better thoughts. Thoughts that inspire you. Thoughts that energize you and invigorate you.

By the time you eventually return to your problem, you may decide that it's not even worth your mental energy. You might even find that it has solved itself, making you glad that you didn't act while you were emotional.

HOW TO DO IT

1. Right now, agree to postpone your thoughts and actions regarding the thing you are

worked up about. Yes... this includes talking. Don't say, do, or think anything about it. You will have time to do that later.
2. Set a limit on how long you will go before coming back to your problem. It could be anywhere from five minutes to twenty-four hours, or whatever you think is appropriate. Note: give yourself more time than you think you'll need, because you don't want to return prematurely. People often think they are calm long before they really are.
3. Try to restore your balance by doing what calms you.
4. Return to your problem once you are no longer feeling strong emotion.

15. THE GRUDGE-DUMP

The "Gist" of it: In this exercise, you are attempting to find calmness by consciously letting go of any resentment you may be holding.

Why it's important: This is an important exercise because forgiveness promotes emotional and psychological well-being -- in us and in those we forgive.

To understand the power of forgiveness, it may be best to look at how your emotional well-being is affected when you choose ***not*** to forgive. You end up ruminating over offenses. You get fixated on retaliation. You are distracted, and you keep friction alive between you and your perpetrators. This keeps them on guard, making them more likely to act defensively toward you. Is your grudge really worth holding?

As you've probably heard, forgiveness means "Setting the prisoner free, and discovering that the prisoner was you." Hannah Moore has said that "Forgiveness is the economy of the heart... it saves the expense of anger, the cost of hatred, the waste of spirits." These are the emotions that are driving us when we're worked up, which is why forgiveness can be such a powerful tool in helping us calm down.

One recent study equates forgiveness to a wonder drug, leading to lower levels of psychological tension in close relationships. It affects the body, lowering blood pressure, strengthening the immune system, improving cardio health, and even alleviating depression. These effects lower a person's risks of certain serious illnesses that are linked to unforgiveness -- cancer being one of them.

I think it's safe to conclude that forgiveness is a sufficient way of calming down -- especially if the thing that is upsetting you is another person's words or actions. Right now, you can experience the calming effects of forgiveness -- no matter what you're doing. No matter where you are. Even if you're not upset with anyone in particular. Even if what you're upset about is something that isn't anyone's fault.

HOW TO DO IT

1. Think of an offense that has been done against you.
2. Recognize how any bad feelings associated with that offense may be making you unhappy and recognize how you will be better off letting go of those bad feelings.
3. Forgive that person who did them -- not for that person's sake, but for yours. This unlocks the cage that is keeping you a prisoner.
4. Once you have done this, find other things to forgive. Focus on being at peace -- even though things around you may be in disharmony. Even though others may have discord and unforgiveness in them. Take charge of the one small part of the chaos that you can control -- your own.
5. Repeat again if necessary until you start to feel just a little bit lighter, a little bit softer, and a little bit calmer.

Note - If you aren't currently upset at anyone, you can look back to an earlier time in your life when somebody wronged you. Focus on forgiving that old transgression now. You may even choose to forgive someone you've already forgiven, being that forgiveness is ongoing. Even after you've done it once, you usually still have to do it again. This will dramatically increase your odds of calming down.

16. THE INVITATION

The "Gist" of it: In this exercise, you are moving towards your bad emotions. You are inviting your anxiety and even welcoming it, rather than fearing it or trying to escape it.

Why it's important: It's important because our anxiety tends to shrink when we face it. When we move toward it, we gain confidence and a sense of self-control.

As you've probably noticed, your survival rate in life has been pretty good so far. You've never actually died from being worked up. Sometimes, it has felt like you were going to die, or as though the world was going to end. But it never did... did it? No. A lot of those bad emotions were only bluffing!

So, as a way of combating them, you can face them. You can call them on their bluff. You can turn towards your fear and anxiety right when they are strongest. Don't back down. Look them in the eye, and say, "Oh, really? Is that all you got? Please give me more."

When you face it and demand more, the paradoxical move pops your anxiety like an over-filled balloon. You are doing the exact opposite that it compels you to do. It is a bit like escaping a Chinese finger trap. Rather than pulling your fingers apart (which is instinctive), you are pushing them toward each other, and the trap loosens.

Stop resisting your emotions. You'll quickly find new strength to handle them. As one Japanese proverb says, "The bamboo that bends is stronger than the oak that resists."

By welcoming your anxiety and your other tough emotions, you are making yourself flexible. And, taking away the only power that those bad emotions have over you. The power to make you angry. the power to make you afraid.

HOW TO DO IT

Face your anxiety. Welcome it. Welcome all of the bad feelings that are tempting you to overreact or to run in the other direction. Face them. Ask them if they have any more that they would like to give. Hold out your hands to show your willingness to accept more. Don't back away. Instead, double down. Like a bad poker player, your frustration will fold as you raise the bet.

You may even try talking to your anxiety verbally. Tell it that it is welcome to stay. Tell it that you aren't going to resist it in any small way. You will most likely find it losing its power to keep you worked up and feeling cornered.

Do this as often as your anxiety returns. If it comes back, think "Oh, hi! Welcome back. Are you going to be staying? That's fine if so. You can stay, while I go about taking care of other priorities." Do not try to escape it. Remember that it is the guest that doesn't like being welcomed.

17. THE PLANNER

The "Gist" of it: In this exercise, you are basically coming up with an action strategy to solve your problem.

Why it's important: It's important because it helps you forge an actionable path toward improvement, which can greatly set your mind at ease.

Forming a plan can benefit you in many ways. For one, it gives you a productive task that is actually deserving of your time and energy. It's far better to think about solutions than it is to let your mind run amuck with upsetting thoughts.

A plan helps you to define your problem. And, by giving it definition, it reduces the unknown, which in turn reduces anxiety. But perhaps the biggest way a plan helps you is the way it improves your life practically. The mental energy you give yields practical dividends. The emotional improvement that follows is merely a byproduct of this.

A plan also reduces your likelihood of making bad choices, which lessens the amount of cleanup work you'll have to do later (as well as the amount of upsetness you'll feel later). So, if you're feeling frustrated and bothered about something right now, I advise you to start forming a plan.

HOW TO DO IT

1. Try to name what is bothering you. Can you define it? Put it into the simplest possible terms.
2. Remove any and all sarcasm, emotional expression, and personal biases.
3. Once your problem has been clearly defined and stripped of unnecessary wordage, try to find just one or two practical steps you can take towards solving it. They can be large

steps or small steps. Ones that start now or ones that start later.

4. Think about any resources you can utilize to help you accomplish this. Is there anyone you know who can help? Are there any books you can read that would better equip you?
5. Create a schedule for those steps -- one that involves precise actions at precise times. The more specific you can be, the better.
6. Bonus: if you're feeling brave, share your plan with a wise person who knows you and who you trust. Allow that person to critique your plan. Revise as necessary.
7. If you're able, begin taking action.

PHYSICAL EXERCISES

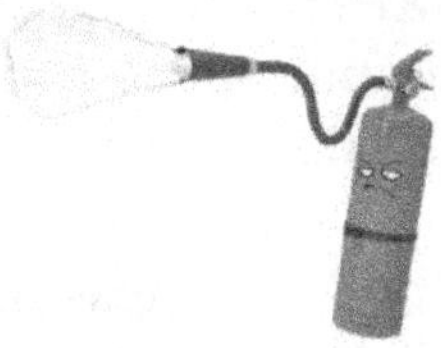

The following exercises have an effect that is primarily physical. While some of them may include psychological aspects, they require more than merely using your brain. Some require you to break out a pen and paper or a guitar, which are things that you cannot do while you're sitting at the dinner table or stuck in traffic. Therefore, the effectiveness of these remedies is contingent upon circumstances, more than it is contingent upon one's ability to focus.

That is both a strength and a weakness -- a strength, if you are someone who struggles to pay attention. A weakness if your immediate environment prohibits you from being able to do what these exercises require.

18. THE ACTION TAKER

The "Gist" of it: This is simply about doing something about your problem. Preferably, something that you've been avoiding.

Why it's important: Taking action is important because it gets you out of your head and into life, affecting your practical world in tangible ways.

It has been said that idleness is the enemy of a peaceful mind. Doing nothing makes us susceptible to aimlessness and unchecked thinking. But, if we are engaged in some activity, our attention and energy have a focus and that susceptibility decreases -- especially when we are doing something that is directly related to our problem. We attack the chaos that is attacking us.

Action protects us from physical and emotional clutter. We clear off our plates when we eliminate any small task. Also, this gives us one less thing to feel worked up about, and usually provides us with a positive distraction. If you're doing something that requires focus, you're too occupied to give much attention to how you're feeling. In a way, taking action is like tricking yourself into becoming calmer.

Taking action is a bit like exercise. It utilizes our minds and our bodies, promoting relaxation. As

David Allen says in his bestselling book, *Getting Things Done*, “Your ability to generate power is directly proportional to your ability to relax.”

To go even further, taking action gives our minds the assurance that we are doing something about our problem. It provides us with the evidence that steps are being taken to solve our problem. This alone works wonders to calm our racing minds.

HOW TO DO IT

Try to focus on one task that you have power to accomplish. It is better if the task is one that is related to the problem at hand, and even better if it is something that you have been putting off for a while. This will add to the amount of emotional weight that is lifted by completing the task.

Next, simply take action. It may be as simple as taking your first footstep on a treadmill. Or, it may involve sorting through that stack of papers on your desk that's been stressing you out. Whatever the case, simply doing something is a great way to start calming down.

If you still do not feel any calmer after you have taken action, continue to take actions until you do. Move from first steps to second steps, and so on, until you are making serious progress with the task at hand.

Even if you do not experience any noticeable calming effect, you will be making progress at something else that is important.

19. THE HUMAN TOUCH

The "Gist" of it: This exercise is simply about being face to face with another person.

Why it's important: It is important because face-to-face interaction is crucial for our emotional well-being. It does more for us than text messages, social media, or talking over the phone.

Acclaimed Psychiatrist and author, David C. Burns, believes that we too seldom rely on the power of human interaction, and instead seek our therapy from self-help books. This is to our disadvantage -- especially in more extreme cases of anxiety, where one-on-one time with another human could truly benefit us.

While Dr. Burns is referring to professional therapy, the benefits he speaks of can come from most forms of human interaction. For example, meeting for coffee with your sister to talk about how you are feeling. Going for a walk with a good friend and telling him about your recent anxiety. Even though you aren't sitting down with a professional, you are getting therapeutic benefits that a self-help book can't give.

These benefits include:

- *Immediate feedback and responses.*
- *The ability to offer empathy and assurance in non-verbal ways, such as through facial gestures and body-language.*
- *The ability to read and reciprocate another person's expressions quickly and effectively.*
- *The ability to make eye-contact when speaking and listening.*
- *The ability to be in close contact with someone that you know and trust.*

All of these benefits are stronger in one-on-one interactions than in scenarios where we are alone or trying to communicate from a distance. Face-to-face communication is a remedy that you can use to calm down right now.

HOW TO DO IT

Right now, try to find somebody that you know and trust to sit down with. It works best if you can find a place that is quiet and without distractions. Next, simply talk. Allow the other person to listen. Do your best to paint a portrait of how you are feeling. Make sure you are rightly conveying your emotions, trying not to leave out unpleasant details or sugar-coat them to make them sound better.

Then, allow the other person to speak. Let her share her thoughts. Be open to what she says. And, try to be present in the conversation, rather than thinking about your frustrations or about what you'll say when it's your turn to talk. Do this until you can tell that it is having a positive influence on your mood.

20. THE BREATHER

The "Gist" of it: This exercise is about giving special focus to your breaths -- their rate, depth, and quality. By doing this, you are able to affect your mood.

Why it's important: This is one of the simplest, most effective, and most convenient ways to calm down -- no matter where you are.

Here is one exercise that is truly portable. You can do it anywhere -- even when you're sitting in your office, just after reading a frustrating email about how the new tariffs will affect your business. Even when you're at home, sitting on the edge of your seat, wondering if that important call is going to come in. Even when you're on the train, riding downtown for that big job interview.

A good portion of modern material places a strong emphasis on breathing. Dan Harris talks about it in his book, 10% happier. Dr. John Gottman speaks of it in a number of his marriage and relationship books. In fact, the majority of anxiety books talk about the relationship between mood and breathing.

At first approach, the topic of breathing may not seem too earth-shattering. It may even sound a little corny -- like something you'd hear about in a meditation audio course, explained by a soft-spoken voice that's just a little too monotone and relaxed. But the thing is... it works! There is actually some good science to back it up.

One paper, published by Science magazine, speaks of a study done on mice, recognizing a connection between the arousal centers of the brain and nerves that regulate breathing. These nerves tell the rest of the body how to react -- whether they should take defense or take rest. The basic conclusion was that calming your mind is about as simple as calming your breathing.

Personally, it took me a few skeptical attempts before I felt convinced. Now though, I can honestly say that this exercise is useful for calming an anxious mind. The results are enough to convince me that there is indeed some significant value to this.

HOW TO DO IT

Simply focus on your breathing. If you're walking, look for a park bench. If you're at work, sit still at your cubicle or go to the break room. If you're at your in-laws, go lock yourself in the bathroom for a few minutes.

Focus on your breaths. Make sure that each breath is deep and regular. Make sure that you are inhaling and exhaling with ease, and that each breath is full. Try to release any tension you may be holding in your torso or your stomach. As you do, try to give your full attention to your body, making sure your breaths are consistent and that your mind stays focused. You should begin to feel a sense of calmness as you regulate your breathing.

21. THE MELODY MAKER

The "Gist" of it: In this exercise, you are using music to help you calm down.

Why it's important: It is important because music can have a powerful influence on emotions.

We usually don't think about how a simple song can affect us, but the influence can be very strong. Researchers in Montreal found that the brain releases dopamine during moments of musical enjoyment, revealing positive physiological and psychological effects.

Music affects the parasympathetic nervous system, promoting relaxation. It can help relieve anxiety and prepare us for sleep. One report stated that people who listen to music tend to fall asleep faster, stay asleep longer, sleep with less interruptions, and feel more energized when they wake.

We know that music can actually calm respiratory and heart rates. In some cases, it has even been shown to lower blood pressure. Maybe, this common tool could help YOU calm down during your emotionally heightened situations.

Don't listen to music that fuels your anxiety. Death metal and hard rock probably won't do the trick. Go to something that you know is capable of taming your anxious mind. Slower. Softer. The kind that you could fall asleep to. Of course, you could always make the music yourself!

If you play an instrument, turn to it when you are upset. Making music gives you an outlet for your emotions. The focus and control required automatically reduce anxiety. And, the physical coordination required calls upon both sides of the brain to work together.

If you are in a situation where you have no music to listen to, or you have no instruments to play, then you can simply sing or hum. Did you know? Singing and humming have been shown to drastically reduce anxiety during fearful, intimidating situations. It improves airflow between the sinuses and the nasal cavity. It gives you something other than your worries to focus on. It is a comfort that many turn to.

HOW TO DO IT

Start by finding a nice, quiet place. Preferably, one where you can sit or lie down. If you are driving, then you may want to pull over. If you are jogging or biking, then you can combine the relaxing effects of exercise with the relaxing effects of music.

If you happen to be preoccupied with some type of responsibility, then you may want to plug in some earbuds to drown out any unwanted background noise. Go to your calming, quieting playlist, and press play. Listen. Allow yourself to be influenced by the strong, calming sounds you hear.

If you would rather play an instrument, simply find a place where you will be able to do so without being bothered (and without bothering anyone else). Shut the door. Focus on the music. Allow yourself to get carried away to a more relaxing place.

22. THE RUB

The "Gist" of it: This exercise uses massage to achieve an effect that is emotionally, psychologically, and physically calming.

Why it's important: It is important because our bodies tend to get pretty tense and rigid when we are worked up.

In fact, "Tense" and "Rigid" are words that we use to describe a worked up person. When we're upset, we tend to stiffen. Our postures display aggression. We may resemble a dog -- ready to attack. Others notice it. But, even more significantly, we feel it. It affects us, whether we are aware of it or not.

When this happens, we can turn to the calming, soothing effects of massage -- whether done by another person or by ourselves. Either way, there are benefits to be gained by loosening our muscles and, consequently, our minds.

While massage may not seem like a practical solution, it offers many practical benefits -- mentally, physically, and emotionally. It can do wonders for our bodies, helping to keep stress, anxiety, and depression at bay.

Massage is known to:

- Lower cortisol.
- Release endorphins.
- Release trapped emotions. And, consequently, it can:
    - Improve sleep.
    - Sharpen the mind.
    - Decrease heart rate.
    - Lower blood pressure.
    - Improve immune system function.

When done by another person, the effects of massage can be even greater. Physical touch has been said to inspire positive thinking and help build trust. It has been thought to reduce stress and anxiety, as well as increase immune function. These are important aspects to our well-being, and ought to be considered when contemplating solutions.

HOW TO DO IT

If you are alone, or if your significant other happens to be far away (or, if that person happens to be the one you are upset with), then there is quite a bit that you can do on your own. As it turns out, you don't need a second person present in order to receive a massage: Even when you are by yourself, you can massage:

- The pressure points in your hands.

- Your palms.
- Your calves.
- Your stomach.
- Your neck.
- Your temples.
- Your sinuses.

If you have a tennis ball, you can rest your body weight on it, using it to massage the arch of your foot, your heel, your hips, your shoulder blades, and your lower back.

A lot of these are things that you can do anywhere. Anytime. Even when you're sitting at your desk, talking on the phone to that unbearable client. Even when you're lying in bed, wondering if your company will be downsizing soon.

If you are upset right now, take a moment to try one of these massage exercises. As you do it, try to focus on releasing your tension. You can combine this exercise with music, if it suits you. Or, you may work better with silence. You may even try to find some positive, affirming thoughts to meditate on while you do it. The more exercises you use, the better your attempts to calm down will typically be.

23. THE FIDGET SPIN

The "Gist" of it: In this exercise, you are basically letting your hand (or foot) stay active, using some type of instrument, such as a tension squeezer or fidget spinner.

Why it's important: It's important because it can allow us to dispel nervous energy when we have more important tasks to focus on.

I know what you're thinking... is this for real? Yes. Hear me out. We all squirm when we're nervous. We bounce, twist, or tap our feet. We drum with our fingers or twiddle our thumbs -- sometimes, under our desks so that nobody notices. And, rather than try to fight this, we could direct our nervous energy towards something. A fidget spinner is great for this.

In case you're doubtful, here's an analogy. Imagine that your brain is a group of people driving somewhere in a car. As one person drives, the people in the back start to grow restless. If they get too restless, they may distract the driver. So, the driver can give them a game to play with each other so that they have something to do while the driver focuses on the road. Similarly, by giving your body a simple, menial task, you can keep your mind from going in unproductive directions.

Consider also how movement, even in small amounts, can be beneficial. For example, office workers gain physical benefit by occasionally getting up from their desks and going for a walk. This is partially for the sake of getting exercise, but also, for the sake of breaking up their monotony. Too much stillness can start to feel imprisoning, hampering creativity and productivity in the mind.

Moreover, think about how physical movement can offer familiarity. In otherwise uncertain situations, it can be calming to do something you are used to doing -- if only to remind you that there is some small thing you still have control of. That is how this mini ritual can actually have a productive purpose.

HOW TO DO IT

Place fidget spinner between two fingers. Spin. Repeat as needed.

Note: Other objects can easily do the same thing, such as tension squeezers or a tennis ball. It is not so important which object you use; it is important that you have something that works for you -- especially if you have other things to take care of that need your full attention.

24. THE REPEATER

The "Gist" of it: This exercise uses the repetition of a powerful or meaningful phrase to bring you confidence, calmness, and clarity.

Why it's important: It is important because it interrupts our negative thought patterns and reinforces thoughts that we want strengthened.

Do you remember those grade school days when someone would misbehave, and the teacher would make that person write a single sentence over and over on the chalkboard? What was the point of that? Yes, it was a form of punishment. But it was intended to do even more. It was an attempt to program a certain thought or principle into that student's mind by way of repetition.

Focusing on one thought or phrase can make something more significant to us. It can make lifeless information come alive, turning it into something that has new meaning. If you could use a better mood and perspective right now, this is a great way to do it.

Maybe it seems a bit cheesy to you. You've watched *What About Bob* too many times, and all you can think of is Bob Wiley repeating to himself that phrase, "I feel good, I feel great, I feel wonderful." Don't let that get you discouraged. If you find this funny, remember that the truth often makes the best comedy!

If you want to calm down, you need something other than your current frustrations being repeated. Try putting on a new record in your mind and letting a more positive message be repeated. Reinforce the good while letting the bad fade. It's basically the opposite of what you're doing now!

Which principle or concept would you really like to have strengthened? Which thought brings you calmness and serenity? You can choose to give that thought power -- right here. Right now. You can choose to make something good even more significant to you -- right when you need it most!

HOW TO DO IT

Try to think of a positive phrase that inspires you or makes you happy. It could be that phrase your grandmother used to tell you -- "this too shall pass." Or, it could be a certain Bible verse that you've memorized -- one that makes you feel centered and balanced.

It could be something that reminds you that the world is bigger than your frustrations, and that time is greater than the current moment you're in. Once you find your phrase, repeat it to yourself over and over -- silently or out loud. Let it become bigger to you than your frustrations. More significant than your bad emotions.

It may not feel like it is helping you at first, but I encourage you to be patient. Trust that the exercise is helping -- even if the effects aren't noticed right away. Eventually, you will begin to see the effect. And, you will start to feel calmer. If you haven't yet done so, give it a try! Make note of how much different you feel once you've started to sense a change. Let that be an inspiration to you the next time you get yourself into another frustrating situation like this.

25. THE MEDITATION STATION

The "Gist" of it: In this exercise, you are using meditation to bring focus and presence.

Why it's important: It is important because it is easy for us not to be mindful of all that's going on around us.

Now, hold on. I know what you're probably thinking. When you hear the word "Meditation," you mind instantly jumps to Eastern religions or New-Age philosophies. That is not what we're talking about here. We're basically just talking about pausing and reflecting. Truly being present. Truly being in the moment. And, doing what we have to in order to get there, using breathing, silence, and deep focus.

Miriam-Webster says that to "meditate" is to "Engage in contemplation or reflection." One might say that it's the act of giving attention to what all five senses can take in. Exiting the thought world and examining the real world.

Meditating is simpler than it is complex. More than it is about holding on or trying to grasp new concepts, it is about letting go of unproductive thoughts and distractions -- much like dumping out the stale water in a glass so that the glass can be filled back up with good, fresh water. While this all may sound simple, I do not mean to make it sound easy, because it's not.

As Dan Harris says in his book, 10% Happier, meditation is actually quite difficult. But, that's just because we rarely do it. As he also says, "if you waited your whole life to go running, you'd find that brutal, too. The first time you try to play an instrument, it's really hard. It's a new skill. Meditation is not relaxation. It's not sitting there and zoning out. You're taming your mind. It's hard work -- just the way rock climbing or swimming a mile is. But it has benefits just like those activities do."

HOW TO DO IT

Step 1: Find a place where you can be free of distractions, if possible. This could be the basement, a bedroom, or your mother-in-law's laundry room, if that's the best you're able to do for the time being.

Step 2: Make yourself comfortable. Basically, choose a position that works for you -- one that doesn't require lots of energy to stay in or cut off circulation to other body parts.

Step 3: Clear your mind. Do your best to focus on the silence and on your breathing. Let the outside world slip away. You may want to close your eyes.

Step 4: Now, just be. That's right -- simply relax and be where you are -- with your sensations. With what's present.

After you have done this for about five minutes, you should begin to feel much calmer. If you find your mind wandering, or feel that it's too difficult to stay focused, you may want to try counting. Start by going from twenty all the way down to zero. Do it slowly. This simple exercise should help you clear your mind. And, it should help give you the calmness that you could really use right now. Give it a try!

26. THE BUILDER

The "Gist" of it: in this exercise, you are simply doing something constructive which will have a positive impact on your emotions.

Why it's important: it's important because building promotes a positive mindset.

I remember when I got my first car. At the time, I barely knew how to change a spark plug. I drove it like it was a toy. When I was excited, I punched the gas. When I was angry, I zoomed around corners. Then, after about a year, the clutch gave out. I told my dad, and he offered to help me replace it.

We were soon lying on our backs beneath the car, staring up at a complex configuration of nuts and bolts -- getting greasy and covered in rust. I started to see that this thing I once thought of as a toy was really quite complex. It was an eye-opener for me.

With each splotch of grease that landed on my shirt, I was finding new appreciation. New value for all of the careful attention that went into this old machine. When I finally started driving it again, I no longer wanted to punch the throttle or go heavy around corners. Even when I was angry, I still wanted to take care of it. I maintained a repairman's mindset. I believe, this is the magic that comes from building.

When you build something, you gain an appreciation for its complexity. Your focus is on seeing it improve, not destroyed. You want to protect it. You want to preserve it.

It is the opposite of how we so often feel when we are angry, ready to do our worst damage to the people and things around us.

By choosing to build something, you are setting yourself up for success. You are doing something that gives you a constructive mindset when you are probably in desperate need of one. Because, when you are building something, even something small, that mindset carries over into other areas of your life.

You have positive energy, and you want it to spread to as many places as it can. You lose your desire to punch walls and hurt feelings, because it goes against your desire to keep on building.

This is one of the most powerful things you can do when you are upset.

HOW TO DO IT

Look for something to build. Anything. It could be big. It could be small. It could be literal, or it could be figurative. It could be your relationship. It could be a promise you've broken to yourself, and that you'd like to repair. It could be that wobbly table that just needs a matchbook under its leg.

You could choose to build your education by going and learning something new. You can choose to build a healthier life by eating the broccoli in the fridge. You can choose to build a better environment by picking up that litter on the side of the road. Any small thing you do to build something will have a subtle impact on your mood. And, the contagious effect should cause it to carry over to other areas in your life, making you more conscientious overall. And, making you calmer.

Repeat the building process over and over as needed. Do it until you no longer feel the desire to use destructive language, actions, or thinking.

27. THE SCRIBBLER

The "Gist" of it: This exercise involves grabbing a pen and a piece of paper (or a computer) and capturing your thoughts.

Why it's important: It is important because writing helps you define your emotions, which can be very calming and therapeutic.

It has been said that our minds have about 50,000 thoughts per day. Many of these thoughts are positive and productive. And yet, quite a few are stressful, fearful, and uncertain. For these negative thoughts, there is a simple, positive, approach -- writing them out.

Writing is an effective therapy for many people. They say they find that when they write their thoughts out, it helps them understand how they are feeling. It helps expose the fallaciousness or the validity in their ideas.

Perhaps, this is because writing involves stillness and reflection -- both of which are helpful in promoting relaxation. And, being still requires a certain amount of focus and steadiness, which quite naturally puts you into a calmer state of mind.

Writing can also give you some valuable insights about yourself. It can help you see where you may have strayed from logic and reason, or where you may have formed unproductive patterns. And, it can help you discover valuable solutions. It is a bit like stepping away from your situation and seeing it from above.

Are you feeling worked up now? Have you tried sitting down with a pen and some paper? If not, I recommend that you try it. This exercise has enormous potential.

HOW TO DO IT

Find a pen and a piece of paper. Or, you can use a digital device of some kind -- a phone, a tablet, or a computer. Just be careful if you do, so that you don't get distracted and forget what you sat down to accomplish.

Now, try to write out what you are thinking and feeling as well as you can. Give a name to your emotions. This may seem silly, as though you are pointing out the obvious. But that is the point. A lot of times, when we are worked up, the obvious is what we can't see.

Write at least a few sentences about what you are feeling. Then, read it to yourself. Do you notice any ways that your own thoughts and feelings may need editing? Can you see where lines of logic have been crossed? If so, document it. As you do, you should notice a growing sense of clarity and an increasing sense of calmness.

INTENSE PHYSICAL EXERCISES

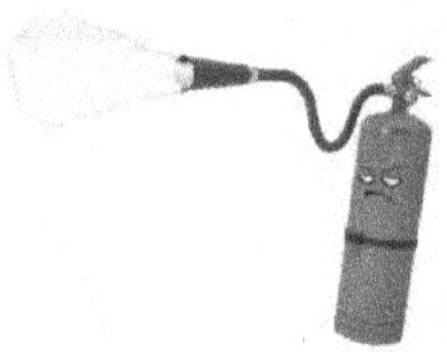

The next set of exercises are more physically intense in their nature. They aim at getting your heart rate up or at getting you to stretch out of your comfort zone. While there are no exercises that offer a guarantee of calming you down, these would be the exercises that come closest to doing so.

Rigorous physical exercise encourages normalization of your body's chemical and hormonal balances. Or, to say it another way, it's actually pretty difficult to stay worked up after doing physically intense exercise.

All the same, I still encourage you not to base your approach on a single method. Your best bet for calming down should contain exercises that are both physical and psychological. Please remember to combine the following exercises with psychological exercises as well (and supplemental, if that is what works for you).

Keep in mind that you can often do physical and psychological exercises simultaneously. While you're on the treadmill, for example, you can also be practicing gratefulness or forgiveness or many of the other psychological exercises. So, if you're doing an intense workout, you might as well pick one of the psychological exercises from the list. By combining exercises this way, you're even more likely to achieve the desired result.

28. THE SWEAT BREAKER

The "Gist" of it: This is a way of calming yourself by doing something physical that increases your heart rate and works out your muscles.

Why it's important: It's important because exercise is one of the most effective ways to balance and stabilize our emotions.

In a Princeton study, researchers injected mice with a substance to mark certain cells. Some of those mice were then placed in an environment that contained running wheels and various kinds of exercise apparatus. The rest of the mice were not given the means for exercising.

When presented with stressful stimuli, the experimenters discovered that the stress didn't last as long in those mice that had the means to exercise. They showed more boldness, curiosity, and confidence than the sedentary mice. It was as though exercise had made them stronger -- physically and mentally. The conclusion: Mammals are better equipped to handle emotions when they are active, rather than sedentary.

Exercise increases the activity of endorphins -- neurotransmitters that reduce pain perception and create a sensation of euphoria. Exercise also increases the concentration of norepinephrine, which has similar attributes to many antidepressants. Further, it causes the physiological systems to communicate with each other, thus increasing their efficiency. In other words, you can begin to calm yourself right now simply by partaking in some form of intense physical exercise. This can include:

- Pushups.
- Sit-ups.
- Pullups.
- Jumping Jacks.

- Squats.
- Cardio workouts.
- Weightlifting.
- Jump-roping.
- Bike riding.
- Jogging.
- Nearly any physical activity you can think of.

HOW TO DO IT

Simply throw on your shorts or sweatpants. And, a t-shirt that you don't mind getting sweaty. Go to the gym if you can. Or, stay at home and keep your jeans and flannel shirt on. There is plenty you can do that doesn't require changing, leaving home, or owning fancy equipment.

29. THE YOGA MAT

The "Gist" of it: This exercise uses yoga as a way of calming down.

Why it's important: It's important because yoga is known to have calming effects on the body and mind.

This is one of those exercises that's a little harder for me to write about, being that I don't really practice it. I also have somewhat of a mental barrier towards it, being that I've always associated it with Eastern Religions that I also don't practice or believe.

However, some of my Christian friends have helped get me past these barriers, assuring me that the benefits of yoga are great, and that it is an altogether separate thing from any religious or philosophical ideologies. In other words, you can practice yoga strictly for its physical and psychological benefits.

So then, what exactly is yoga? One definition describes it as "breath control, simple meditation, and the adoption of specific bodily postures, widely practiced for health and relaxation." As a calming agent, we might say that yoga works under one simple principle -- we can control our emotions by controlling our bodies.

To get you started, I have included two of the most common beginner exercises below, should you attempt to combat your frustrations with this exercise.

HOW TO DO IT

A. Child's Pose

If you are not experienced with yoga and aren't sure how to begin, the "Child's Pose" is a good place to start. You start by kneeling down with your knees straight in front of you (about hip-width apart from each other). Let your toes touch.

Now, inhale and exhale slowly. As you exhale, lean forward, resting your body on your thighs and allowing your forehead to touch the mat in front of you. Stretch your arms straight forward, resting your palms down on the mat before you.

As you do this, try to let your back muscles soften. Let the tension in your neck, arms, and shoulders drift away. Keep your eyes closed and focus on your breathing. Do this until you start to feel more relaxed.

B. Warrior 1

Here is how you start: put your right leg forward and your left foot back -- almost towards the back of the mat. Keep your right leg in front of you in such a way that your knee is in front of your heel, but not your toes. Does that make sense? If not, you may want to find a video on this. Anyway, lift your arms straight up. Face forward as you proceed. Allow your thoughts to settle.

As you do this, focus on your breathing, your thoughts, and your posture. Keep your hands on your hips, doing your best to keep them straight/square. Allow your thoughts to balance and re-center.

HERBAL SUPPLEMENTS

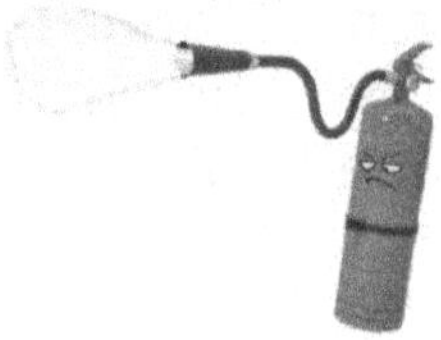

This final category includes vitamins or supplements that you can take which have been known by many to have a calming effect.

30. HERBAL SUPPLEMENTS

The "Gist" of it: in this exercise, you are simply doing something constructive which will have a positive impact on your emotions.

Why it's important: it's important because many people swear by the effectiveness of using herbal remedies to calm down. However, a lot of it seems to depend on the person. While one person may notice significant effects from a remedy, another person may notice none. It will probably have a lot to do with your own personal wiring and sensitivity.

Let's talk about some of the main herbal remedies that people find helpful:

Kava Kava

This supplement, also known as *Piper methysticum*, is sometimes recommended for mild cases of anxiety. It comes in various forms, such as tablets or tea drinks. It works as a muscle relaxant, carrying over its effects to the brain. It is said to leave the user relaxed, but alert.

Some say that kava helps them achieve tranquility on sleepless nights or during busy, stressful seasons at work, allowing them to calm down and work steadily. Others say that it helps them cope with the daily stresses of life, or that it simply allows them to kick back and watch a movie on Saturday night. Many people also say that the effects are fast-acting. However, none of this should be taken as medical advice. You should talk to your physician before deciding if kava is right for you.

It should also be noted that the FDA has issued a warning on kava kava, saying that it can have negative effects on the liver. While it isn't extremely common, and while it has typically only resulted from taking the supplement in excessive amounts, it is all the more reason why you should talk to your doctor before taking kava -- especially if you are known to have any liver-related problems.

Valerian Root

This supplement, also known as v*aleriana officinalis*, is claimed to have positive effects on insomnia, ADHD, menstrual cramping, restless leg syndrome, OCD, dizziness, and digestive problems, among other things. While such claims have not been approved by the FDA, this does not necessarily warrant automatic dismissal.

Valerian root is available in many forms. It comes as tablets, tea, powder, and liquid extract. It has often been combined with St. John's wort or lemon balm. It is also often combined with melatonin to tag-team the effects of insomnia.

You should do your own research about valerian root and consider that there are some cautions linked to it. It is said to cause some side effects in people, such as headaches, upset stomach, and mental dullness. Some people report feeling extra sluggish upon waking.

Valerian root is another supplement that you should not take if you have liver problems. Or, if you are pregnant. Be aware that it may also interact other drugs, such as antihistamines, barbiturates, antidepressants, narcotics, and benzodiazepines.

St. John's wort

This supplement comes from a plant found in nature. It has five petals, star-shaped, yellow flowers, and it typically grows to be about 2-4 feet tall. It is most commonly used as a mood booster, as well as for nervousness, tiredness, and poor appetite. Some have even used it for symptoms of menopause as well.

While reported to be no more effective than a placebo in cases of extreme depression, there is said to be some strong scientific evidence existing backing the supplement's effectiveness for treating mild to moderate depression. Unfortunately, however, we still know very little as to whether there are any long-term effects.

St. John's wort comes in powder, tablet, tea, and liquid extract forms. The most common of these is tablets, which are often taken in doses of two, two times a day (or with meals). Some brands recommend that the supplement be taken for at least two months in order to gain the maximum benefit. It can also be made into an oil to treat skin wounds;

however, some have reported this making their skin extremely sensitive to sunlight.

As a caution, please keep in mind that St. John's wort might cause serious interactions with some medications, such as birth control meds or antidepressants. Because of this, it is only available with a prescription in some countries. France has actually banned its use in French products. Again, it is always wise to talk to your doctor before deciding to take any new supplements or medications.

If you are interested in finding out more about other existing supplements, I have composed a short list below, which you can use to begin your own research. The following supplements have also been said to have calming characteristics:

- **Passionflower**
- **Eucalyptus**
- **Lavender**
- **Impatiens**
- **Star of Bethlehem**
- **Cherry Plum**
- **Rock Rose**
- **Clematis**
- **Bach's rescue remedy**
- **Homeopathy, including (but not limited to) *Aconitum*, *Arsenicum album*, *Phosphorus*, *Lycopodium*, *Gelsemium*,**

and *Argentum nitricum*. There are many others to look into as well.

TEN IMPORTANT VIRTUES, PRINCIPLES, AND TRAITS THAT SUMMARIZE THIS BOOK

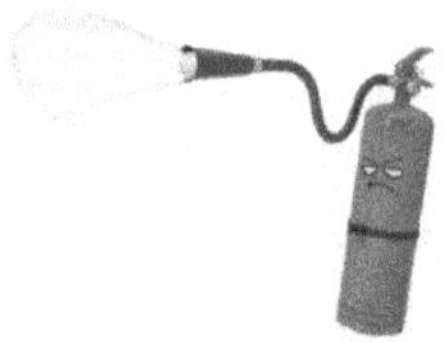

As one of the final sections of this book, here are 10 important traits, skills, and principles that basically summarize this book. They bring together everything we've been talking about so far. By choosing to focus on (and grow in) these areas, you will also be strengthening your ability to become calmer.

#1. ATTITUDE

A short time ago, I was on a business trip in Denver. I arrived late to my hotel and waited for the receptionist to check me in. However, after pressing a few buttons on her keyboard, she turned to me and said, "Sorry, your name isn't in our reservation list." Then she turned and walked away.

I wasn't sure if she was coming back. If not, she hadn't really given me much information to go by. I saw her take a seat in the back room and pull out her phone, either texting a friend or shopping on Amazon. I decided to call for her again. I said, "Excuse me, but could you please help me figure this out? I have an important meeting in the morning, and I am already going to be missing out on sleep." She looked at me with disgust, saying, "Sir, what part of this don't you understand? You're not in the system. That's all there is to it. Good night!"

I was offended, but even more, shocked. It threw me off to be talked to by someone whose job was be of service. I was a guest. I had paid for a room. What part of that did SHE not understand? Feeling about ready to lose my cool, I went outside for a breath of fresh air. I needed to try to contain myself.

After a few minutes thinking, I came back inside. I looked the rude receptionist square in the eye, and said, "Listen, miss... I don't appreciate you talking to me like I'm roadkill. Here in America, smart businesses know that they should treat customers with respect. Have you ever heard of America? Have you ever heard of respect? Have you ever heard of customers? Guess what... that's me. I'm your customer!"

She looked at me like I was an alien, and said, "Excuse me, sir, but I've done all I can for you. I even went way out of my way for you earlier, and this is the thanks I get?" Again, I was stunned by what I was hearing. Not knowing what else to do, I pulled myself together, bit my lip, booked a different room, and went straight to bed. Lucky for both of us, I was too tired to share my real thoughts.

It was only a short time later when I was on another business trip, having a much different kind of experience. I ended up waking up after the cafe had closed, missing breakfast by just a minute. I gently knocked on the café door to ask if there were any leftover apples or muffins that they didn't mind parting with.

A woman came to the door and gave me a huge smile. She welcomed me in and insisted that I sit down. I tried to refuse, but she demanded that I take a load off while she brought back out all the food she had just put away.

I almost felt guilty. I wasn't used to being treated so well by anyone. Why was this woman being so magnanimous? Why was she willing to do all this extra work for me, even though I was just a stranger to her? It made me feel like I wasn't a stranger -- like I was more of a family member... a son or a nephew.

As I sat there in my seat, she brought out a large plate of biscuits, gravy, eggs, bacon, and hash browns -- piping hot. I wondered if I was still dreaming. I sat back and ate like a king, feeling grateful and completely satisfied.

I truly felt touched by this woman's kindness. I walked away feeling good. Not just about her, but about myself. About humanity. I felt a rekindled faith in people overall. Perhaps that sounds like an exaggeration, but it's not. It's really how good I felt.

On my way out, I walked up to the secretary and told her what a fine job my server had done. I left some kind words and a twenty-dollar bill, along with a positive review on the hotel's website. The review simply said, "Thank you... for making me feel so welcome."

I've often thought about how different these two experiences were. In one, I was treated like a trespasser -- a nuisance who not much good could be expected of. In the other situation, I was treated like royalty. A prodigal son welcomed home from wandering. What could account for such drastically different experiences? I eventually realized... it was attitude.

One woman's attitude was totally negative towards me. She viewed me as a bother, and that's all I ended up being to her. The other woman's attitude was positive towards me, and I ended up being very positive towards her.

The ironic thing is that they both got exactly what they were expecting. Neither of them were wrong! In my mind, this is a sign that we should be careful what we expect from people. Because, it seems that we so often get exactly what we think we are going to get -- good or bad. So, we might as well have good expectations!

You can probably also learn something about yourself here by examining the people you are surrounded by. If you're surrounded by warm, loving people, it might say something about your attitude. If you're surrounded by cold, confrontational jerks, it also might say something about your attitude.

How does this relate to calming down? Well, since a good majority of life's upsetting moments involve other people, we could each learn to improve our attitudes towards those people. Because, we tend to get what we expect -- from people and from life!

#2. TIME MANAGEMENT

Another principle that is directly related to calming down, is time-management. This is where a lot of our stress comes from. Since many of us aren't good managers of our time, our lives become way more stressful than they need to be.

An example of this would be financial debt -- since many of us are stressed out by it, we ignore it. But that doesn't cause it to go away. It causes interest to add on. It causes our debt to transfer over to debt collectors.

Our growing problem may even give us a sense of shame. Of course, this only makes us even less likely to face it. More prone to overreacting whenever the problem surfaces. The more time that passes without properly managing our responsibilities, the greater our stress levels.

In the book, "Eat That Frog," author Brian Tracy says that we should start out our day by facing the biggest, most daunting task first. If the least-desirable task we have planned is to "Eat a frog," well then... that's where we should begin. Doing this makes the remainder of our day less daunting, as the least desirable aspect of our day has already been achieved.

Time management is a subject that many books have been written about. But, for most of us, it can probably be summed up with just three simple words: dealing with discomfort. The better (and quicker) we are at facing tough obstacles, feelings, and responsibilities, the better off we are as people -- emotionally and psychologically.

The problem is that procrastination is a pretty subtle foe. Many of us don't know we're doing it. We trick ourselves into doing pointless busy work that seems productive but isn't. We may spend minutes or hours rearranging our email inboxes, satisfied by the illusion that we are making progress, when we are really just neglecting what we ***should*** be doing.

Perhaps, you know firsthand that when you have a tough job to do, anything else sounds better. You suddenly become interested in things that you normally don't care about. You came to YouTube to find answers to a certain problem, but two hours later, you're still there -- watching videos about how whales communicate. How does this happen?

It happens by telling ourselves one small lie -- that the unfavorable task we are avoiding now will sound more appealing to us later on. It's a lie, and we should know this by now. History constantly shows us otherwise. Every time we put something off for tomorrow, we still find ourselves wanting to wait just one more day. This is the sour fruit that is born of procrastination.

It usually hurts us in two ways. One, it keeps us from doing something productive. Two, it often causes us to partake in behaviors that don't really edify us in any way. This is the case when you know you have a report due tomorrow, but you instead find yourself eating ice cream, watching a marathon of reruns on Netflix.

Learning good time-management will improve your overall calmness. By quickly addressing whichever problems you can, you are indirectly addressing your internal problems as well. As they say, clutter on the outside means clutter on the inside. By taking care of that clutter on the outside (which requires good time-management), you indirectly take care of the clutter on the inside.

It's just one more area you can focus on, that will have a positive overall effect on your emotional reactivity.

#3. TEAMWORK

We tend to get worked up in situations that involve other people. These situations account for a good majority of our lives. Usually, the people we want to work with are the same ones we are frustrated by.

This includes our wives, our siblings, our children, our coworkers, and our friends. So then... why is it that some of our most frustrating moments involve these people?

Perhaps, because these people are nothing like us. They don't think like us. They don't see the world the way we do. Their ways of communication differ from ours. At first, we may have been drawn to these differences, but over time, these differences can frustrate us. They can irritate us. They can challenge our ability to think and function. We may find ourselves asking, "Is it worth it to be on a team?"

Teams work under the belief that the group is greater than the sum of its parts. Of course, this fun phrase doesn't really account for how much patience is required to be a part of the group. Some of those "group parts" are quite difficult to work with. Some of them have idiosyncrasies and quirks, making them hard to talk to. They make it easy to doubt that group work can be more beneficial.

But success isn't about being the smartest, the strongest, or the fittest. It's about being adaptable. Flexible. It's about being able to roll with the punches. If you've ever watched a team-survival show, you've seen that some of the most independent people give up sooner than anyone. And, some of the people who make it to the end are the ones who didn't seem like good bets at the start. What is the one factor that so often sets the winners apart from the losers? An ability to work well with others.

Throughout life, we find ourselves in situations that can be improved by being part of a team. As children, in school, at home, and at work. Our marriage success depends on cooperation. Our business lives depend on cooperation. Most of the big decisions we make in life involve other people. It is crucial for us to know how to put our differences aside and work together.

Sadly though, many of us have never cultivated good people skills. We've never made it a priority to be valuable teammates. Instead, we are comfortable with our own methods of getting through life. We'd usually rather do a job ourselves than trust somebody else to help us.

A lot of this has to do with personal insecurity. We are afraid to let others too close. We like them being just distant enough to keep them from seeing our flaws. We cling too tightly to the images we want to maintain of ourselves. As we grow less interdependent, we become more isolated. More needy. And, our levels of social anxiety increase.

We would be far better off learning to capitalize on the goodwill of others. Because, somewhere deep down, every human being wants connection. And, every human being sometimes needs a hand. Being a part of a strong team helps to meet both of those. If we have good teammates, we are rarely without help. And, if we have good help, we have one less reason to get worked up.

#4. COMMUNICATION

There is a funny irony that occurs when we are worked up -- the greater our state of need, the worse we tend to be at communicating. The more frantic our behavior becomes. The more jumbled our words flow out of our mouths. The more our neediness comes across as aggression, and the more we chase away those people who we were depending on for our rescue.

This is exactly why it is so imperative that we learn to communicate effectively. Especially when we are worked up. This tends to be when our state of need is greatest, and we would most benefit from having the assistance of other people. Knowing how to communicate with them helps to ensure that they will work -- not against us, but for us and alongside us -- advancing us closer to our goals.

Focusing on calm communication will make you a better teammate, because being a good teammate requires knowing how to talk to your team. It presents the need to state your requests, voice your concerns, and discuss relevant matters.

Many of us fail to do this -- not because we are incapable, but because we haven't yet taken the first step, which involves processing. How can a person express his thoughts and feelings if he doesn't first know what they are?

Thinking is an important step in communication. Knowing what we want makes us more skilled at asking for it. Knowing what we feel makes us better at expressing it. Knowing what we think makes us better at explaining it. As Albert Einstein once said, "If you cannot explain it simply, you don't understand it well enough."

This is the problem that many of us have in our relationships. Since we aren't really sure of our own message, we aren't good at delivering it. We use unclear language. We use sarcasm, hints, or other forms of indirect communication. Or, we may get worked up, resorting to shouting and yelling.

It's so easy to raise our voices and hope that the people around us will notice us and give us what we need. And yet, all this usually does is cause people to avoid us. It causes them to evacuate the scene, fearful of our tones and expressions.

We don't have to scream at the people in our lives in order to get what we want from them. If they care about us, they'll probably come to our aid voluntarily. If not, the problem usually isn't on their end. It's on our end. It usually means we haven't communicated our needs well enough.

Don't yell at your kids when you need help. Don't throw a fit when you want your husband to get off the couch and start working. Talk to these people. Make your requests clear. Make your frustrations clear too. But, do it calmly. The better you are at communicating calmly, the more likely others will be to help you get what you need. And, the less reason you'll have to get worked up.

#5. RESILIENCE

Throughout our lives, most of us have heard others say, "If at first you don't succeed, then try, try again." Or, "If you fall off your horse, get back on it." Such sayings are so common that they almost lose their meaning. But they are telling us something valuable. It's common for us to fall. And, common for us to want to stay down after we've fallen.

Resilience is the word that describes one's quality to get back on his horse. It is often referred to as "bouncing back." Author Brene Brown says that it's all about a "Tolerance for discomfort." Because, no matter how many times we've fallen before, it hurts just as much the next time, and the next time after that.

It seems fair to ask, what is this discomfort that we should build up a tolerance for? Perhaps, the better question is, "What are our unhealthy forms of comfort?" Video games and old reruns of LOST? Alcohol or chocolate ice cream? No doubt, certain comforts of ours point directly to certain discomforts that we are escaping.

Decreasing some of these comforts can help us develop a thicker skin. And, consequently, give us an advantage in nearly all areas of life -- in our relationships, jobs, and personal lives. We'll be better students if we're able to stick with it when things look bleak and never-ending. We'll be better parents if we're able to handle it when our kids reject us. We'll be better employees if we're able to learn from our mistakes and reevaluate our commitment, rather than sink into silent surrender.

By becoming "tougher," we will be making ourselves more well-rounded. Less fragile. Less susceptible. And, if we are able to reach a place where life's abrasions don't have such a strong impact on us, we will be better at staying calm as well.

#6. OWNERSHIP

As we've discussed in this book, blame is a very common barrier standing between many people and their happiness. It keeps them focused on external factors, rather than looking inside to see the problems they actually have power to change.

They think their unhappiness points to circumstances, things, or people, and they turn to those people and things as outlets for their aggression. While this provides them with an instant sense of relief, it doesn't make them happy.

Because, to be happy, we must own our stories. We must acknowledge the parts of our lives that are lacking and admit the role we've played in making things how they are. We may be at fault in great or small ways.

Of course, we aren't responsible for everything that happens to us in life, because a lot of it is beyond our control. We can easily err on the side of taking too much responsibility -- not just for ourselves, but for others as well.

Lately, you've been bearing the weights of your husband, who still counts on you to wake him up every morning. And, your kids, who still think it's your job to do their laundry (even though they're old enough now). Not only is this unfair to you, it's unfair to them.

It's noble to care for them, but you can actually interfere with their joy and development. They need to own their stories too. They need to develop more mature, responsible habits too. Are you helping that process, or hindering it? Be careful not to bear crosses that aren't yours.

Consequence is a strong teacher. But it cannot teach if you're not letting it. Take responsibility for yourself. Let others do the same. And, remember that your problems are -- first and foremost, yours. Owning them is part of being happy. And, better tempered.

#7. PATIENCE

Patience is a virtue, as it is often said. It's the one that links directly to so many of life's frustrations. When we're waiting for the bathroom. Waiting for a slow gas pump. Waiting for an indecisive driver to pick a lane. Little things seem like big things. We get antsy and irritable. We snap at the people around us. We disrupt vital processes that would improve our life quality.

In his book, Twelve rules for life, author Jordan Peterson talks about a case study in which patience played a vital role in certain rats' abilities. The experimental rats learned how to do some incredible things. But it took lots of time. And, patience. The point of the story was that patience can help us draw great things out of ourselves. And, each other.

It would be great if we didn't have to wait for progress to occur. If we could metamorphose from caterpillars to butterflies overnight, awaking to find that we make more money. We run a quicker mile. We are closing bigger sales. Whatever the case, progress takes time. Whenever we want to make a change in our habits or our attitudes, we have to be patient with the process, as well as with ourselves.

Many of the people we admire for being great are often the same people who have the resolve to see something across the finish line. Patience is yet one more trait that will improve the quality of our lives. And, make us calmer people overall.

#8. ACTION

It's a funny thing, but we tend to like ideas better in principle than in practice. When it comes to difficult things like dieting, exercising, or learning a new healthy habit, ideas fascinate us. But when it actually comes to actually practicing these ideas -- we suddenly lose our interest. We suddenly wonder what on earth made us feel so inspired to make such a ridiculous commitment.

When it actually comes time to pass on a cheeseburger and order a salad instead. When it comes time to spend your free time running, rather than watching your favorite TV show. When it comes time to put your money into an IRA, rather than spend it on a new flat screen TV. Suddenly, the ideas that interested us are no longer interesting.

We all love good principles when they are ideas. Few of us would object to the fact that that exercise is beneficial. Few of us would reject the notion that healthier food is more energizing. We might even get inspired just thinking about these things. We might even commit to a plan to integrate them into our lives. This would require zero effort. But what would require effort is making a plan work.

When it comes to calming down, the same is true. Many of us love the idea of staying in control when our spouses are pushing our buttons. We like the idea of learning how not to flip the crazy switch when we are on our way out the door for church. But, when these situations actually present themselves, we suddenly find ourselves being steered by our emotions, rather than by the principles that once inspired us.

Feelings seem to be our strongest motivating force. Many of us rely on feelings to tell us what to do, where to go, what to buy, and what to eat. The thing is, feelings don't really matter much. At least, not in a practical sense. What matters is our actions.

What makes you strong isn't how you feel about going to the gym; it's actually going to the gym. It's actually picking up a pair of dumbbells until your shirt is soaked in sweat. What makes your cardiovascular health improve isn’t the way you feel about the treadmill. It’s the way you actually get on the treadmill and ignore your feelings. Real results are about what you do; not what you feel. Remember that the right feelings don’t even have to be present to do the right actions.

As a rule of thumb, first do what you know is right. Then, worry about finding inspiration. Chances are, you’ll be done before the inspiration even comes. And, once you do finish the difficult task, you’ll be feeling inspired -- simply because you did it! Don’t just be a person of ideas; be a person of action.

#9. REALISM

Have you ever wondered why your crazy switch gets flipped during certain situations? When you’re heading out the door for church. When a big holiday is just a day away. When an anniversary or birthday comes. When you are leaving for a vacation. Why is it that some of the most stressful moments are the same ones that you had high expectations for? Maybe, there is something here worth noting.

It seems that real life has a hard time matching our expectations. The higher our expectations are, the more likely reality is to fall short in comparison. And, the more likely we are to be bummed about the drastic difference.

Learning to form more realistic expectations is another thing that can decrease our overall anxiety. If we can allow ourselves to have more reasonable expectations, we won't be so devastated when things don't go exactly as we hoped.

Your drive to work won't be ruined by some guy cutting you off in traffic. Your anniversary won't be ruined by your husband checking the football score during dinner on his phone. Your drive to church won't be a disaster when you realize that the kids just aren't hustling quickly enough to get out the door.

Why not? Because these were all realistic expectations that you were factoring in. And, because you were factoring them in, they lost their power to upset you.

#10. CONGRUENCE

The other day, I had to take my daughter's toy away from her. She was throwing a fit, and I told her that she could have her toy back once she settled down. But, when I took the toy, she surprised me. She said, "I don't want it, daddy. You can keep it." What surprised me was that I knew it wasn't true.

I knew for a fact that that toy meant a lot to her. Somehow, she was actually able to change her own mind. In order to avoid the discomfort of losing something, she convinced herself that it wasn't really a loss.

But this clued me in to a certain rule that each of us seems to unknowingly live by. We need congruence between our reality and our thinking. When our reality and our thinking aren't aligned, we either have to alter something in reality so that it aligns with our thinking or alter something in our thinking so that it aligns with reality. If there is incongruence, we are miserable.

An example of this would be if your doctor diagnosed you with morbid obesity and told you that it was affecting your health. Naturally, you would find this news unpleasant. But you would also find it forcing you to make a choice. Either you could change something in reality or change your thinking about reality.

Changing your reality might look something like this: you get a gym membership. You cut back on fast food. You start drinking more water. You do things that help make your reality better. Or, you could change your thinking, which might look something like this: you tell yourself that that doctor is full of it. You tell yourself that it doesn't matter. You tell yourself that you don't mind being obese. Either way, you are restoring congruence between reality and your beliefs.

Some realities, we cannot change -- such as the reality that all humans are mortal. Every one of us must come to grips with the fact that we will not live forever. Our only choice in the matter is to change our thinking, because we cannot change this reality.

The point is to realize that we are always striving for congruence, whether by altering reality or altering how we see it. The right choice isn't always obvious, as the serenity prayer makes clear - "LORD, give me the strength to change what I can. The grace to accept what I cannot. And, the wisdom to know the difference."

Because, we are all capable of accepting things we shouldn't accept and choosing our beliefs -- not on the basis of how true they are, but on the basis of how convenient they are. Anytime we find ourselves tempted to change our thinking; we should see it as a warning sign. And, a good time to stop and inspect our motives.

How might this apply to you? Have you allowed yourself to believe that certain faults or imperfections are just part of who you are, when they may not really be? Could you be doing more to change your life for the better than you've allowed yourself to believe is possible? You should at least consider this. And, pass up convenience for something better. Choose what's right -- even if it's harder now.

CONCLUSION

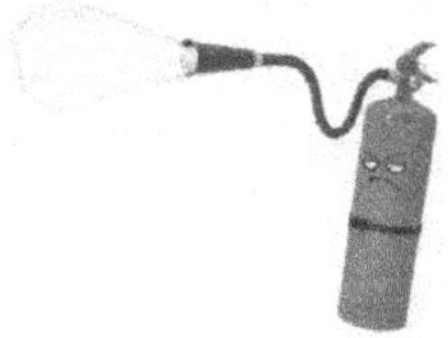

Congratulations. You've made it to the end. I hope you've enjoyed reading this book. I hope it has addressed the topics that are pertinent for you and provided you with some viable solutions. Ultimately, that has been the goal.

A lot of the advice I've shared is simple. It may even seem too simple. I have been careful not to oversimplify the problem, yet I know that simple truths and facts are what we seem to need constant refreshers of. Most often in life, when we are hurting ourselves in some way, it is because there is some simple truth that has gotten away from us which we need to be reminded of.

Please... take these simple truths to heart. Apply them. Just because something is simple, doesn't mean it won't require your time and effort. The effectiveness of these techniques depends on how long and how hard you work at them. I dare you NOT to take the blamer's route, criticizing this book for ways in which you fail to benefit by what it teaches.

If you find that you are tempted to throw this book into the cellar or use it to stabilize the wobble in your table, then I have a request: please consider rereading the crucial chapters. Please consider giving what you've read a second try and doubling down on your efforts. Change takes more than reading a book once. It takes effort and time.

Now, as you head back out into life, bring the helpful bits of knowledge that you've learned with you. When you find yourself tempted to lose it again, press pause. Step back from this situation. Try to see things from a different angle. Do something that calms you down. Reread the lists you made at the start of this book. Be smart enough to recognize your own patterns and tendencies at work.

Keep in mind how bad that feeling of regret is to taste, and let it serve as a reminder when you are tempted to take another mouthful. Remember the look of hurt in your loved one's eyes each time you've spoken to them harshly or without a filter. Save yourself from repeating the additional embarrassment and headache. Work to preserve your dignity and your credibility.

If it helps, get some fresh air. Be alone. Take a pause from the fast pace of life and focus on what matters -- your relationships. Your job. Your finances, and all those good things that you still have. Your peace of mind is precious -- worth holding onto at all costs.

THE END

ABOUT THE AUTHOR

Hey all,

My name's Caleb. Great to meet you. I am a father, husband, musician, and writer of self-help books, relationship books, and Christian non-fiction books, which I sometimes give away for free on my website, **www.authorcaleb.com**.

While I do a lot of sharing about myself, I would love to talk more with you about your interests! Feel free to email me with any questions, comments, compliments, or complaints. My email address is **Newbooksforyou@Hotmail.com**. I'll do my best to respond in a timely manner. Or, please subscribe to my newsletter, which you will also be able to do on my site. This is another great way for us to stay in touch, and for you to receive the latest news on free books and music offers!

Finally, please take a moment to review this book. For a writer, reviews are like little drops of golden sunshine that bring warmth and happiness... especially when they have GOOD things to say (which is something I can only hope for; not demand). So, as a writer who LOVES writing and wants to STAY writing, your review will be greatly appreciated. Come on... just head over to Amazon. It'll take you a minute! And, it will make me feel like I've just gotten a hug!

Well, that's all for now. Thanks again for your time, support, and interest. I look forward to our next encounter!

Sincerely,

Caleb

ALL BOOKS BY CJ KRUSE

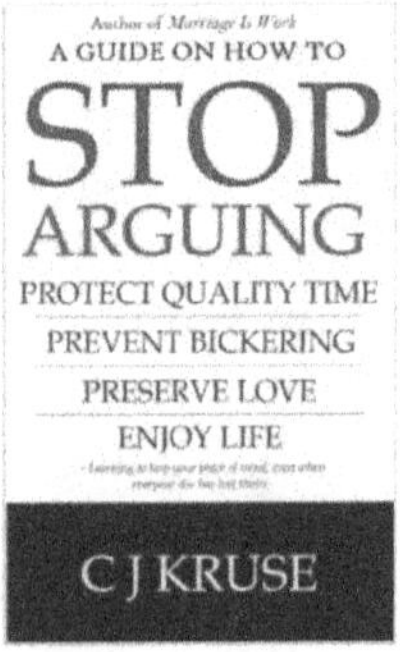

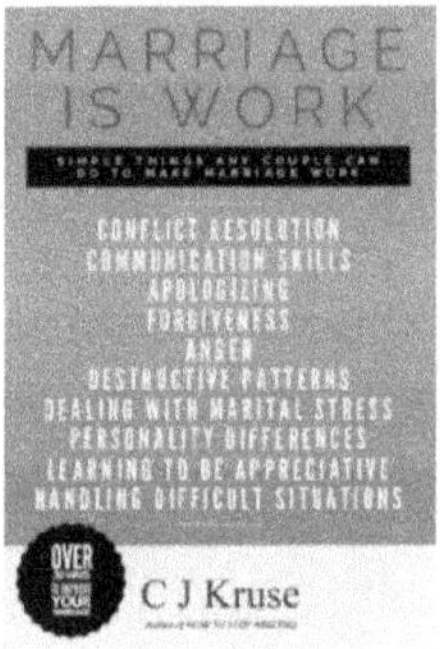

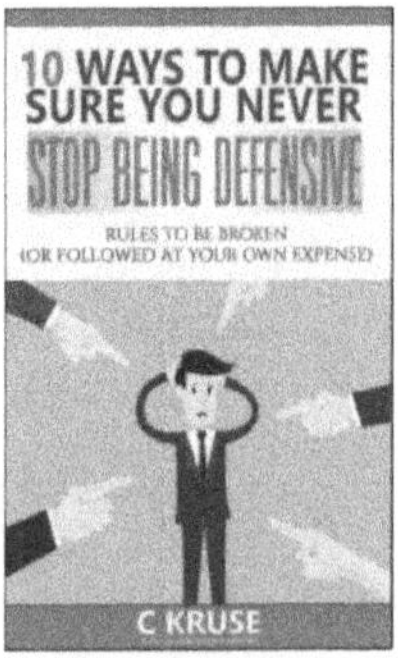

10 WAYS TO MAKE SURE YOU NEVER
STOP BEING DEFENSIVE
RULES TO BE BROKEN
(OR FOLLOWED AT YOUR OWN EXPENSE)
C KRUSE

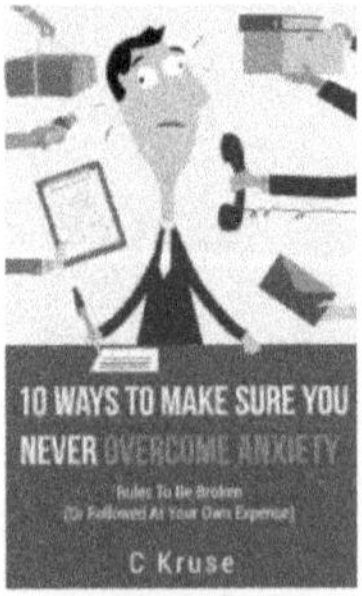

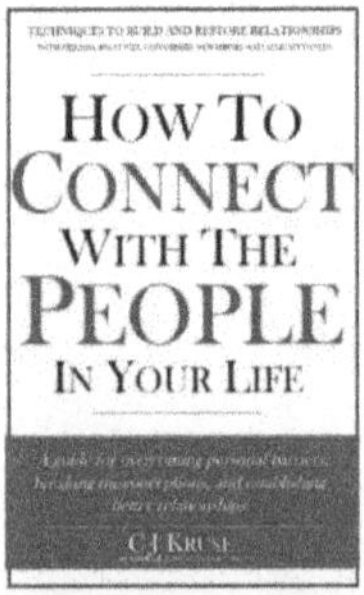

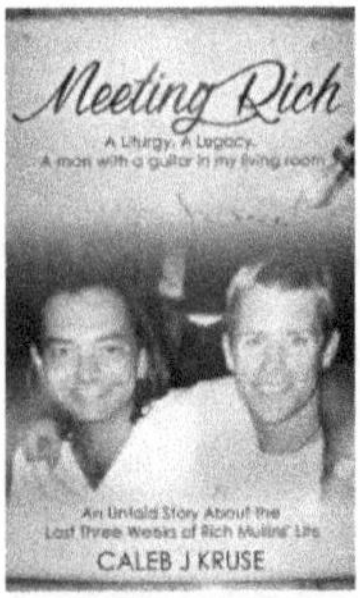

Meeting Rich
A Liturgy. A Legacy.
A man with a guitar in my living room
An Untold Story About the Last Three Weeks of Rich Mullins' Life
CALEB J KRUSE

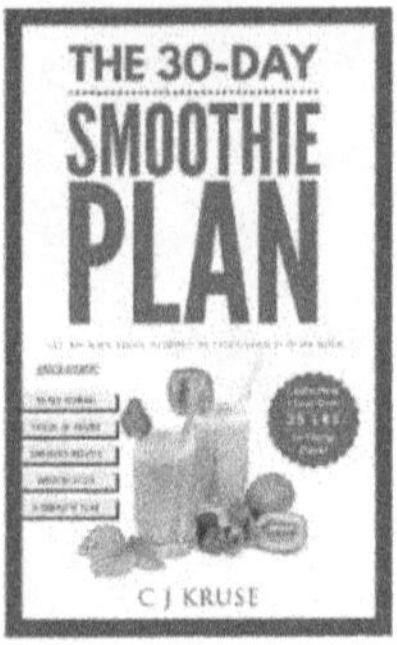

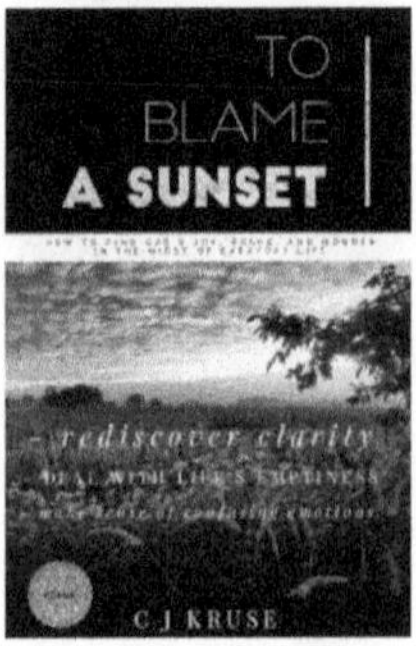

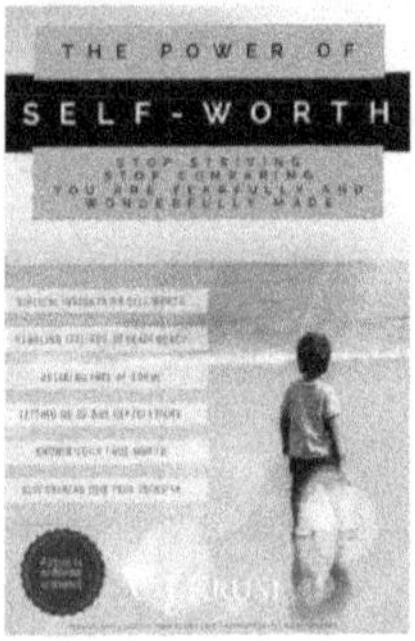

THE POWER OF
SELF-WORTH
STOP STRIVING
STOP COMPARING
YOU ARE FEARFULLY AND WONDERFULLY MADE

www.ingramcontent.com/pod-product-compliance
Lightning Source LLC
LaVergne TN
LVHW091251080426
835510LV00007B/221
9781951028107